History of the Architecture of Kashmir

A book for UG 5th Semester History Q&A

Dr. Khalid Bashir

pencil

ISBN 978-93-5667-851-4
© Dr. Khalid Bashir 2023

Published in India 2023 by Pencil

A brand of
One Point Six Technologies Pvt. Ltd.
Unit no. 26, Ground Floor, Building A1,
Wadala Truck Terminal Road,
Near Post Office, Antop Hill, Mumbai - 400037
E connect@thepencilapp.com
W www.thepencilapp.com

Author biography

Dr. Khalid Bashir, a distinguished scholar and senior Assistant Professor, is the Head of the Department of History at Government Degree College Sopore. With 18 research papers and six notable books, including "The Foundation of Muslim Rule in India: A Look at the House of Slave Rulers" (translated into French, Spanish, and Italian), his expertise in Kashmiri culture and heritage is unparalleled. Dr. Khalid's passion for history and extensive knowledge make him an exceptional guide, unraveling the mysteries of Kashmir's architectural wonders. His dedication and scholarly achievements provide readers with a comprehensive exploration of the region's rich heritage, enriching our understanding of this remarkable cultural legacy.

CONTENTS

Preface

I am extremely excited to introduce the book titled *"History of the Architecture of Kashmir"* to history students who are looking for a thorough resource to aid them in their exam preparation. While creating this book, my main objective has been to address exam-oriented questions and provide well-crafted answers, aiming to offer students a well-organised method of studying archaeology.

I would like to express my appreciation for the backing and motivation I received from my colleagues and friends, Mr Nisar Ahmad Khan of Statistics, Mr Firdous Ahmad Malla of Mathematics, Dr Wasim Akram Zargar of Information Technology, Mr Sajad Ahmad Inspector JKP, Dr Fayaz Hussain Asst. Prof. Histiory GDC Katra, Mr. Iqbqal Shafi Sharegojree and Dr Mohammad Ashraf Khawaja. Throughout the process of writing this book, my colleagues and friends have been incredibly supportive. Their insightful input and feedback have been indispensable in ensuring that the content aligns with the needs of students studying "History of the Architecture of Kashmir" as their skill paper in the fifth semester of their undergraduate program.

The book is structured into ten chapters, specifically designed to cover the key topics that students are likely to encounter in their exams. Within each chapter, a comprehensive explanation of the core concepts is presented, supplemented with illustrative examples. This approach aims to facilitate students' understanding of the material and enhance their preparedness for the exams.

I aspire for this book to be a helpful resource for History students, enabling them to excel in their exams and gain a profound comprehension of this captivating field of study. I extend my heartfelt gratitude to my colleagues for their continuous support and encouragement in the successful completion of this book.

I wholeheartedly welcome and highly value any suggestions that can further enhance the book's quality.

Chapter-I

Short Answer Type Questions

Q. no.1 What is Medieval Architecture?

Ans. Medieval architecture refers to the architectural styles that were prevalent during the Middle Ages, from the 5th century to the 15th century.

Q. no.2 What is the historical value of Medieval Architecture?

Ans. Medieval architecture serves as a visual representation of the social, economic, and cultural development of the Middle Ages. It reflects the beliefs, values, and aspirations of the people of that time.

Q. no.3 What is the aesthetic value of Medieval Architecture?

Ans. Medieval architecture is valued for its unique features such as pointed arches, ribbed vaults, and flying buttresses. It is also admired for its intricate carvings, stained glass windows, and sculptures that depict religious and mythological themes.

Q. no.4 Why is Medieval Architecture important to study?

Ans. Studying Medieval Architecture helps us understand the cultural and artistic achievements of the past. It also allows us to appreciate the beauty and complexity of these architectural styles.

Q. no.6 What are some famous examples of Medieval Architecture in Kashmir?

Ans. Shah Hamdan Mosque, Pari Mahal, Jama Masjid, Khanqah-e-Moula and Hari Parbat Fort.

Q. no.7 How did Medieval Architecture influence later architectural styles?

Ans. Medieval Architecture had a significant impact on later architectural styles such as Gothic Revival and Renaissance. Elements of Medieval Architecture can be seen in many modern buildings, particularly in churches and government buildings.

Q. no.8 What were some of the challenges faced by Medieval architects and builders?

Ans. Medieval architects and builders faced several challenges, including limited resources, lack of technology, and inadequate tools. They had to rely on their creativity and expertise to construct buildings that were sturdy and aesthetically pleasing.

Q. no.9 What were some of the key features of Medieval Castles?

Ans. Medieval castles were characterized by their thick walls, towers, and moats. They were designed to protect their occupants from enemy attacks.

Q. no.10 What role did religion play in Medieval Architecture?

Ans. Religion played a significant role in Medieval Architecture. Churches and cathedrals were designed as places of worship and reflection. The architecture of these buildings reflected the religious beliefs and values of the people of that time.

Q. no.11 How has the preservation of Medieval Architecture been important?

Ans. The preservation of Medieval Architecture has been important in maintaining our cultural heritage. It allows us to learn from the past and appreciate the achievements of our ancestors. It also provides a visual representation of our history and identity.

Q.no.12 What were some of the popular building materials used in Medieval Architecture?

Ans. The popular building materials used in Medieval Architecture were stone, brick, and timber. These materials were readily available and were used to construct sturdy and durable buildings.

Q. no.13 What was the role of guilds in Medieval Architecture?

Ans. Guilds played a significant role in Medieval Architecture. They were associations of craftsmen who worked together to maintain high standards of workmanship and protect their trade secrets. They also provided training and support to new apprentices.

Q. no.14 What were some of the key advancements in Medieval Architecture?

Ans. Some of the key advancements in Medieval Architecture included the development of pointed arches, ribbed vaults, and flying buttresses. These innovations allowed for the construction of larger and more complex buildings.

Q. no.15 What is the current state of Medieval Architecture?

Ans. Many Medieval buildings still exist today, although some have suffered damage over time. Preservation efforts are ongoing to ensure that these buildings are maintained and protected for future generations to enjoy.

Q. no.16 Write a note on the medieval architecture of Kashmir.

Ans. The medieval architecture of Kashmir is a reflection of the region's rich cultural and artistic heritage. It includes a range of styles, such as Persian, Islamic, and Indian, and features impressive structures like mosques, shrines, forts, and gardens. Some famous examples of medieval architecture in Kashmir are the Shah Hamdan Mosque, Pari Mahal, Jama Masjid, Khanqah-e-Moula, and Hari Parbat Fort. These structures are known for their intricate carvings, elegant wooden architecture, and strategic locations. They serve as a testament to Kashmir's vibrant past and continue to be an important part of the region's cultural identity.

Medium Answer Type Questions

Q. no.1 What is Medieval Architecture?

Ans. Medieval architecture refers to the architectural styles that were prevalent during the Middle Ages, from the 5th century to the 15th century. It encompasses a wide range of architectural styles, including Romanesque, Gothic, and Renaissance, which were characterized by specific design elements, construction techniques, and materials.

Q. no.2 What is the historical value of Medieval Architecture?

Ans. Medieval architecture has significant historical value as it provides a visual representation of the social, economic, and cultural development of the Middle Ages. The architectural styles of this period were influenced by the political and religious climate of the time, as well as by the available technology and resources. The buildings constructed during this period reflect the beliefs, values, and aspirations of the people of that time.

Q. no.3 What is the aesthetic value of Medieval Architecture?

Ans. Medieval architecture has great aesthetic value, as it is characterized by unique features such as pointed arches, ribbed vaults, and flying buttresses. The intricate carvings, stained glass windows, and sculptures that depict religious and mythological themes are also admired for their beauty and artistic quality. The overall effect of these architectural styles is to create a sense of grandeur, majesty, and spirituality.

Q. no.4 Why is Medieval Architecture important to study?

Ans. Studying Medieval Architecture is important for several reasons. Firstly, it helps us understand the cultural and artistic achievements of the past. By examining the architectural styles and techniques of the Middle Ages, we can gain insight into the social, political, and religious values of that time. Secondly, it allows us to appreciate the beauty and complexity of these architectural styles. Finally, it provides a foundation for understanding the evolution of later architectural styles.

Q. no.5 What are some famous examples of Medieval Architecture?

Ans. There are many famous examples of Medieval Architecture, including the Notre Dame Cathedral in Paris, Westminster Abbey in London, and the Colosseum in Rome. These buildings are admired for their beauty, historical significance, and cultural importance. They serve as a testament to the ingenuity, creativity, and skill of the architects and builders who constructed them.

Q. no.6 How did Medieval Architecture influence later architectural styles?

Ans. Medieval Architecture had a significant impact on later architectural styles such as Gothic Revival and Renaissance. The design elements and construction techniques developed during the Middle Ages served as a foundation for the development of new styles and approaches to architecture. Elements of Medieval Architecture can be seen in many modern buildings, particularly in churches and government buildings.

Q. no.7 What were some of the challenges faced by Medieval architects and builders?

Ans. Medieval architects and builders faced several challenges when constructing buildings during the Middle Ages. These challenges included limited resources, lack of technology, and inadequate tools. Builders had to rely on their creativity and expertise to construct buildings that were sturdy and aesthetically pleasing. The use of new construction techniques and materials, such as pointed arches and ribbed vaults, helped overcome some of these challenges.

Q. no.8 What were some of the key features of Medieval Castles?

Ans. Medieval castles were characterized by their thick walls, towers, and moats. They were designed to protect their occupants from enemy attacks. Castles also included features such as drawbridges, portcullises, and battlements to further enhance their defensive capabilities.

Q. no.9 What role did religion play in Medieval Architecture?

Ans. Religion played a significant role in Medieval Architecture. Churches and cathedrals were designed as places of worship and reflection. The architecture of these buildings reflected the religious beliefs and values of the people of that time. Religious themes were often depicted in the decoration of these buildings, with sculptures and stained glass windows depicting scenes from the Bible and other religious texts.

Q. no.10 What were some of the popular building materials used in Medieval Architecture?

Ans. The popular building materials used in Medieval Architecture were stone, brick, and timber. These materials were readily available and were used to construct sturdy and durable buildings. Stone was particularly popular for its durability, while brick and timber were used for their ease of use and availability.

Q. no.11 What was the role of guilds in Medieval Architecture?

Ans. Guilds played a significant role in Medieval Architecture. They were associations of craftsmen who worked together to maintain high standards of workmanship and protect their trade secrets. They also provided training and support to new apprentices. Guilds were particularly important in the construction of churches and cathedrals, as they helped ensure that the buildings were constructed to a high standard.

Q. no.12 What were some of the key advancements in Medieval Architecture?

Ans. Some of the key advancements in Medieval Architecture included the development of pointed arches, ribbed vaults, and flying buttresses. These innovations allowed for the construction of larger and more complex buildings. Pointed arches allowed for taller and more slender buildings, while ribbed vaults provided additional support for the roof. Flying buttresses allowed for greater stability in large buildings.

Q. no.13 What was the significance of Gothic Architecture in Medieval times?

Ans. Gothic Architecture was significant in Medieval times as it represented a shift from the Romanesque style. Gothic buildings were characterised by their intricate decoration and emphasis on vertical lines. They were also designed to allow more natural light into the building. The gothic architecture reflected the religious and cultural values of the time and was used to express the power and wealth of the church.

Q. no.14 What is the current state of Medieval Architecture?

Ans. Many Medieval buildings still exist today, although some have suffered damage over time. Preservation efforts are ongoing to ensure that these buildings are maintained and protected for future generations to enjoy. Many Medieval buildings have been repurposed for modern use, such as museums or government buildings, while others continue to serve their original purpose as places of worship.

Long Answer Type Questions

Q. no.1 What is the historical significance of Medieval Architecture?

Ans. Medieval Architecture has significant historical value as it reflects the social, religious, and cultural values of the time. In the Middle Ages, the church was a central part of daily life, and church buildings were often the most important and impressive structures in towns and cities. The architecture of these buildings, particularly the grand cathedrals, was used to express the power and wealth of the church.

Medieval Architecture also reflects the advances in engineering and construction techniques of the time. The development of pointed arches, ribbed vaults, and flying buttresses allowed for the construction of larger and more complex buildings than had been possible before. The use of these techniques also allowed for the creation of buildings with more intricate and decorative features, such as stained glass windows and elaborate carvings.

Additionally, Medieval Architecture has historical value as it reflects the political and economic structures of the time. Many Medieval buildings, particularly castles and fortresses, were designed for defence purposes. The architecture of these buildings reflects the feudal system, with the lord's residence often being the most impressive and well-fortified structure in the area.

Q. no.2 What is the aesthetic value of Medieval Architecture?

Ans. Medieval Architecture has significant aesthetic value due to its intricate decoration, use of light and shadow, and focus on verticality. Gothic Architecture, in particular, is known for its ornate decoration and intricate carvings. The use of stained glass windows allowed for the creation of a stunning interplay between light and shadow, creating a sense of otherworldliness and beauty.

Additionally, the use of verticality in Medieval Architecture creates a sense of grandeur and awe. Many Medieval buildings, particularly cathedrals, were designed to reach towards the heavens, with soaring spires and pointed arches. This emphasis on vertical lines creates a sense of upward movement and aspiration, reinforcing the religious and cultural values of the time.

Finally, Medieval Architecture also has aesthetic value due to the skill and craftsmanship required to create these buildings. The intricate carvings and delicate stonework required a level of skill and attention to detail that is often lacking in modern construction. The preservation of these buildings allows us to appreciate the skill and craftsmanship of the medieval craftsmen who created them.

Q. no.3 How does the debate on the value of Medieval Architecture reflect wider cultural and historical debates?

Ans. The debate on the value of Medieval Architecture reflects wider cultural and historical debates around the role of history in contemporary society. Some argue that the preservation of medieval buildings is important for cultural and historical reasons, as they represent an important part of our shared heritage. They argue that the destruction or neglect of these buildings would be a loss to our collective cultural memory.

Others argue that the preservation of Medieval buildings is a waste of resources and that these buildings should be allowed to fall into disrepair or be demolished to make way for more modern structures. They argue that the historical value of these buildings is overstated and that they have little relevance to modern society.

This debate reflects wider discussions around the value of tradition and history in contemporary society. Some argue that tradition and history are important for creating a sense of identity and continuity, while others argue that they can be oppressive and limit progress. The debate around the value of Medieval Architecture is an important part of these wider discussions, as it reflects the tensions between tradition and progress and the role of the past in shaping our present and future.

Chapter-II

Very short answer type questions

Q. no.1 What is Parihaspora?

Ans. Parihaspora was an ancient city located in the Kashmir Valley.

Q. no.2 What is the significance of the Martand temple?

Ans. The Martand temple was an important Hindu temple located in Kashmir that was built during the ancient period.

Q. no.3 Who built the Avantisvamin Temple?

Ans. The Avantisvamin Temple was built by King Avantivarman in the 9th century.

Q. no.4 Where is Payar temple located?

Ans. The Payar temple is located in the Anantnag district of Jammu and Kashmir in India.

Q. no.5 What is the architectural style of the Parihaspora?

Ans. The architectural style of the Parihaspora was a combination of Indian and Greek architectural styles.

Q. no.6 When was the Martand temple built?

Ans. The Martand temple was built in the 8th century during the reign of King Lalitaditya.

Q. no.7 What is the significance of Avantisvamin Temple?

Ans. The Avantisvamin Temple is an important temple that represents the architectural style of the Kashmiri dynasty.

Q. no.8 Who built the Payar temple?

Ans. The Payar temple was built during the reign of the Karkota dynasty in the 8th century.

Q.no.9 What was the purpose of the Parihaspora?

Answer: Parihaspora was an important political and cultural center during the ancient period in Kashmir.

Q.no.10 What happened to the Martand temple?

Ans. The Martand temple was destroyed by Muslim invaders in the 14th century.

Q.no.11 What is the architecture of Avantisvamin Temple?

Ans. The Avantisvamin Temple is an example of Kashmiri temple architecture and features intricate carvings and sculptures.

Q.no.12 What is the significance of the Payar temple?

Ans. The Payar temple is an important archaeological site that provides insights into the religious and cultural practices of ancient Kashmir.

Q.no.13 Who ruled Kashmir during the construction of the Martand temple?

Ans. The Martand temple was built during the reign of King Lalitaditya, who ruled Kashmir during the 8th century.

Q.no.14 What is the material used in the construction of the Avantisvamin Temple?

Ans. The Avantisvamin Temple was constructed using stone and brick.

Q.no.15 What is the current state of Payar temple?

Ans. The Payar temple is in a state of ruins and has undergone extensive renovation and restoration work in recent years.

Q.no.16 What is the significance of the Parihaspora in Kashmir's history?

Ans. Parihaspora was an important cultural and political centre during the ancient period and played a crucial role in shaping Kashmir's history.

Q.no.17 What was the purpose of the Martand temple?

Ans. The Martand temple was built as a place of worship for Hindus during the ancient period in Kashmir.

Q.no.18 What are some unique features of the Avantisvamin Temple?

Ans. The Avantisvamin Temple features intricate carvings and sculptures, including images of various Hindu deities and mythological figures.

Q.no.19 What is the historical significance of the Payar temple?

Ans. The Payar temple is an important archaeological site that provides insights into the religious and cultural practices of ancient Kashmir and the Karkota dynasty.

Q.no.20 What was the architectural style of the Martand temple?

Ans. The Martand temple is an example of ancient Kashmiri temple architecture and features a distinctive mix of Indian and Greek architectural styles.

Q.no.21 Who was the patron of the Martand temple?

Ans. The Martand temple was patronized by King Lalitaditya, who ruled Kashmir during the 8th century.

Q.no.22 What was the function of the Avantisvamin Temple?

Ans. The Avantisvamin Temple served as a place of worship for Hindus during the ancient period in Kashmir.

Q.no.23 What is the historical significance of Parihaspora's architecture?

Ans. Parihaspora's architecture represents a unique fusion of Indian and Greek architectural styles and reflects the cultural diversity of ancient Kashmir.

Q.no.24 What is the present condition of Martand temple?

Ans. The Martand temple is in ruins, with only the remnants of its walls and pillars remaining.

Q.no.25 Who built the Payar temple?

Ans. The Payar temple was built by the Karkota dynasty during the 8th century.

Q. no.26 How did Lalitaditya Muktapida's extensive military campaigns impact the art and architecture of ancient Kashmir?

Ans. Lalitaditya Muktapida's extensive military campaigns had a significant impact on the art and architecture of ancient Kashmir. The vast resources he acquired through his conquests allowed him to commission many impressive construction projects, including the Martand Sun Temple. However, the constant warfare and instability of his reign also led to a decline in artistic and architectural output in the later years of his rule.

Q. no.27 What is the significance of the Martand Sun Temple in the context of ancient Kashmiri architecture, and which ruler was responsible for its construction?

Ans. The Martand Sun Temple is one of the most significant examples of ancient Kashmiri architecture, renowned for its intricate stone carvings and delicate stucco work. It was commissioned by Lalitaditya

Muktapida during his reign and remains one of the most impressive and well-preserved examples of ancient Indian temple architecture.

Medium Answers Type Questions

Q. no.1 What are some of the unique features of the Martand temple's architecture?

Ans. The Martand temple is an excellent example of ancient Kashmiri temple architecture, characterized by a unique blend of Indian and Greek architectural styles. The temple's distinctive features include a symmetrical design, intricate carvings on the temple walls, and a central courtyard surrounded by columns.

Q.no.2 How did the Avantisvamin Temple contribute to the development of Kashmiri architecture?

Ans. The Avantisvamin Temple is an important example of Kashmiri temple architecture and reflects the unique architectural style of the Kashmiri dynasty. It features a square base, a pyramidal roof, and intricate carvings of various Hindu deities and mythological figures. The temple's architecture has been influential in shaping the design of other temples in the region.

Q.no.3 What is the significance of the Payar temple in the context of ancient Kashmir?

Ans. The Payar temple is an important archaeological site that provides insights into the religious and cultural practices of ancient Kashmir. The temple's unique architectural features, including its circular design and intricate carvings, suggest that it served as a place of worship for Hindus during the Karkota dynasty's reign.

Q.no.4 What role did Parihaspora play in the development of ancient Kashmiri architecture?

Ans. Parihaspora was an important cultural and political centre during the ancient period and played a crucial role in shaping Kashmir's history. The city's architecture is characterized by a unique blend of Indian and Greek architectural styles, reflecting the cultural diversity of ancient Kashmir. Parihaspora's influence can be seen in the design of other buildings and temples in the region.

Q.no.5 How has the restoration work on the Payar temple impacted its historical significance?

Ans. The restoration work on the Payar temple has helped preserve the temple's unique architectural features and provided a better understanding of the religious and cultural practices of ancient Kashmir. It has also increased the temple's historical significance by making it accessible to visitors and scholars interested in studying ancient Kashmiri architecture and culture.

Q. no.6 What materials were used in the construction of ancient Kashmiri temples?

Answer: Ancient Kashmiri temples were constructed using a variety of materials, including stone, brick, and wood. Stone was the most commonly used material due to its durability and strength, while brick was often used as a cheaper alternative. Wood was also used for decorative purposes and for constructing the roofs of temples.

Q. no.7 What was the significance of symmetry in the design of ancient Kashmiri temples?

Ans. Symmetry played an important role in the design of ancient Kashmiri temples as it reflected the concept of balance and harmony in Hindu mythology. Symmetry was achieved through the use of repeated patterns, columns, and a central axis. It also provided a sense of order and stability to the temple's design.

Q. no.8 How did the architecture of Kashmiri temples change over time?

Ans. The architecture of Kashmiri temples evolved as new rulers brought in new architectural styles and ideas. The earlier temples were simple and had a square or rectangular plan. However, over time, the temples became more complex and featured intricate carvings, sculptures, and decorations. The influence of foreign cultures, such as Greek and Persian, also impacted the architecture of Kashmiri temples.

Q. no.9 What role did mythology play in the design of ancient Kashmiri temples?

Ans. Mythology played a significant role in the design of ancient Kashmiri temples, as it reflected the Hindu belief in the power of the gods and goddesses. The temples were designed to accommodate the different rituals and ceremonies associated with each deity. The carvings and sculptures on the temple walls depicted various mythological stories and legends, allowing devotees to connect with the gods and goddesses on a deeper level.

Q. no.10 What challenges did architects and builders face when constructing ancient Kashmiri temples?

Ans. The architects and builders of ancient Kashmiri temples faced several challenges, including difficult terrain and extreme weather conditions. The mountainous terrain made transportation of building materials difficult, while the harsh winters and hot summers made construction work challenging. Additionally, political instability and religious conflicts often disrupted temple construction projects. Despite these challenges, the architects and builders were able to create some of the most magnificent temples in the region.

Q. no.11 What is the significance of Lalitaditya Muktapida's reign in the context of art and architecture in ancient Kashmir?

Ans. Lalitaditya Muktapida's reign is considered significant in the context of art and architecture in ancient Kashmir because he commissioned several impressive construction projects throughout his kingdom, including the construction of the Martand Sun Temple. He also patronized several artists and craftsmen, which led to the creation of many exquisite works of art and handicrafts.

Q. no.12 How did Lalitaditya Muktapida contribute to the development of architecture in Kashmir during his reign?

Ans. Lalitaditya Muktapida contributed to the development of architecture in Kashmir during his reign by commissioning several ambitious building projects, including the construction of the Martand Sun Temple and the Parihaspora city. He was also responsible for the creation of several new architectural styles that blended elements of Indian, Persian, and Central Asian architecture.

Q. no.13 What are some of the notable architectural achievements of Avantivarman's reign in Kashmir?

Ans. Some of the notable architectural achievements of Avantivarman's reign in Kashmir include the construction of the Avantisvamin temple and several other impressive temples and buildings. Avantivarman was also known for his innovative use of materials and construction techniques, which helped to advance the state of architecture in Kashmir during his reign.

Q. no.14 How did Avantivarman's patronage of art and architecture influence the cultural landscape of ancient Kashmir?

Ans. Avantivarman's patronage of art and architecture had a significant impact on the cultural landscape of ancient Kashmir. His support for artists and craftsmen led to the creation of many exquisite works of art and handicrafts, and his construction projects helped to establish a unique architectural style that blended elements of Indian, Persian, and Central Asian architecture. This legacy continued to influence the artistic and architectural traditions of the region for many years to come.

Q. no. 15 What are some of the unique features of the art and architecture of Kashmir during the reigns of Lalitaditya Muktapida and Avantivarman?

Ans. Some of the unique features of the art and architecture of Kashmir during the reigns of Lalitaditya Muktapida and Avantivarman include the use of intricate stone carvings and delicate stucco work, as well as the incorporation of elements from Indian, Persian, and Central Asian architecture. Both rulers were also known for their innovative construction techniques and their patronage of artists and craftsmen, which helped to establish Kashmir as a centre of artistic and architectural excellence.

Q. no.16 How did Avantivarman's artistic patronage and architectural innovations differ from those of his predecessors and successors in Kashmir?

Ans. Avantivarman's artistic patronage and architectural innovations differed from those of his predecessors and successors in Kashmir in several ways. He was known for his innovative use of materials and construction techniques, and his architecture often incorporated elements of Persian and Central Asian styles in addition to traditional Indian styles. He was also a notable patron of the arts, and his reign saw the creation of many beautiful works of art and handicrafts.

Q. no.17 Can you describe some of the distinctive features of the Avantisvamin temple, and what influence did it have on later architecture in the region?

Ans. The Avantisvamin temple is notable for its distinctive architectural style, which blends elements of Indian, Persian, and Central Asian architecture. It's intricate stone carvings and elaborate roof decorations are particularly noteworthy, and the temple is considered one of the most impressive examples of ancient Kashmiri temple architecture. Its influence can be seen in later architecture throughout the region, as many later temples and buildings incorporated elements of its unique style.

Q. no.18 In what ways did the reigns of Lalitaditya Muktapida and Avantivarman represent high points in the development of ancient Kashmiri art and architecture?

Ans. The reigns of Lalitaditya Muktapida and Avantivarman represented high points in the development of ancient Kashmiri art and architecture for several reasons. Both rulers were known for their patronage of the arts and their innovative approach to architecture, which helped to establish Kashmir as a centre of artistic and architectural excellence. Their reigns saw the creation of many impressive buildings and works of art that continue to inspire and amaze visitors to the region to this day.

Q. no.19 How did the art and architecture of ancient Kashmir evolve during the reign of Lalitaditya Muktapida?

Ans. Lalitaditya Muktapida's reign marked a high point in the development of ancient Kashmiri art and architecture. He was a patron of the arts and commissioned many impressive buildings and works of art, including the famous Martand Sun Temple. The art and architecture of his era were characterized by intricate stone carvings, delicate stucco work, and an emphasis on symmetry and balance. The use of locally available materials such as limestone and sandstone was also a hallmark of this period.

Q. no.20 What were some of the key features of the Martand Sun Temple, and what made it such an impressive example of ancient Kashmiri architecture?

Ans. The Martand Sun Temple was one of the most impressive and well-preserved examples of ancient Kashmiri architecture. It was constructed during the reign of Lalitaditya Muktapida and featured intricate stone carvings, delicate stucco work, and a complex layout that emphasized symmetry and balance. The temple was also notable for its innovative use of materials and construction techniques, such as the use of large blocks of limestone and the incorporation of a central courtyard. The temple's impressive size and scale, combined with its intricate detail work, make it a remarkable example of ancient Indian temple architecture.

Q. no.21 How did Avantivarman's reign mark a departure from the artistic and architectural styles of his predecessors in ancient Kashmir?

Ans. Avantivarman's reign marked a departure from the artistic and architectural styles of his predecessors in ancient Kashmir in several ways. He was known for his innovative use of materials and construction techniques, which incorporated elements of Persian and Central Asian styles in addition to traditional Indian styles. His architecture also featured more intricate and detailed stonework than in previous eras, with an emphasis on elaborate roof decorations and ornate stone carvings. Additionally, his reign saw the creation of many beautiful works of art and handicrafts, which helped to establish Kashmir as a centre of artistic excellence.

Q. no.21 What were some of the distinctive features of the Avantisvamin temple, and how did it influence later architecture in the region?

Ans. The Avantisvamin temple is notable for its distinctive architectural style, which blends elements of Indian, Persian, and Central Asian architecture. It's intricate stone carvings and elaborate roof decorations are particularly noteworthy, and the temple is considered one of the most impressive examples of ancient Kashmiri temple architecture. Its influence can be seen in later architecture throughout the region, as many later temples and buildings incorporated elements of its unique style. The temple's impressive size and scale, combined with its intricate detail work, make it a remarkable example of ancient Indian temple architecture.

Q. no.22 How did the reigns of Lalitaditya Muktapida and Avantivarman contribute to the overall development of ancient Kashmiri art and architecture?

Ans. The reigns of Lalitaditya Muktapida and Avantivarman were instrumental in the overall development of ancient Kashmiri art and architecture. Both rulers were known for their patronage of the arts and their innovative approach to architecture, which helped to establish Kashmir as a centre of artistic and architectural excellence. Their reigns saw the creation of many impressive buildings and works of art that continue to inspire and amaze visitors to the region to this day. Their contributions helped to shape the cultural identity of the region and left a lasting legacy in the history of Indian art and architecture.

Long Answer Type Questions

Q. no.1 How did the fusion of Indian and Greek architectural styles influence the development of Kashmiri architecture?

Ans. The fusion of Indian and Greek architectural styles had a significant impact on the development of Kashmiri architecture during the ancient period. The blending of these two styles was evident in the design of Parihaspora, a city in Kashmir that was an important cultural and political centre during the 6th and 7th centuries.

Parihaspora's architecture reflected a unique blend of Indian and Greek styles, with its large collonaded halls and ornate carvings. The city was designed to be a centre of learning and culture, with several temples, palaces, and administrative buildings constructed using this architectural style. This fusion of styles resulted in a unique architectural identity that reflected the cultural diversity of ancient Kashmir.

The influence of Greek architecture can be seen in the use of large columns and colonnades, which were characteristic features of Greek buildings. The Indian style was evident in the intricate carvings and sculptures that adorned the temples and palaces. The fusion of these two styles resulted in a unique architectural style that was characterized by symmetry, balance, and harmony.

The impact of this fusion can also be seen in the design of other temples in Kashmir, such as the Martand temple. The temple's architecture features a central courtyard surrounded by columns, which is reminiscent of the Greek style. However, the intricate carvings on the temple walls and the use of Indian mythological figures and deities in the carvings reflect the Indian influence.

Overall, the fusion of Indian and Greek architectural styles had a profound impact on the development of Kashmiri architecture during the ancient period. It resulted in a unique architectural identity that reflected the cultural diversity of the region and influenced the design of temples and other buildings in Kashmir for centuries to come.

Q. no.2 How did the Payar temple serve as a reflection of the cultural and religious practices of ancient Kashmir?

Ans. The Payar temple is an important archaeological site in Kashmir that provides insights into the cultural and religious practices of ancient Kashmir. The temple was constructed during the 8th century by the Karkota dynasty, which ruled Kashmir from the 7th to the 9th centuries.

The temple's architecture is characterized by a circular design, which was unique for the time. The temple's walls feature intricate carvings of Hindu deities and mythological figures, reflecting the importance of Hinduism in the region during the ancient period. The circular design of the temple may have been influenced by the circular designs of Buddhist stupas, which were also prevalent in the region at the time.

The Payar temple served as a place of worship for Hindus during the Karkota dynasty's reign. The temple's design and architecture reflect the religious and cultural practices of the time, with its intricate carvings depicting Hindu deities and mythological figures. The temple's circular design may also reflect the importance of the sun in Hindu mythology, as the sun is often associated with circular shapes.

The restoration work on the temple has provided valuable insights into the building techniques and construction methods used during the ancient period. It has also helped preserve the unique architectural features of the temple and made it accessible to scholars and visitors interested in studying the religious and cultural practices of ancient Kashmir.

Overall, the Payar temple serves as a reflection of the culturaland religious practices of ancient Kashmir, providing valuable insights into the region's history and heritage.

Chapter-III

Very Short Answer Type Questions

Q. no.1 What are the prominent features of temple architecture in ancient Kashmir?

Ans. The prominent features of temple architecture in ancient Kashmir include the use of stone, wood, and brick, intricate carvings and sculptures, a square or rectangular plan, a pyramidal roof, and a central spire.

Q. no.2 How did the use of stone, wood, and brick contribute to the temple architecture in ancient Kashmir?

Ans. The use of stone, wood, and brick contributed to the temple architecture in ancient Kashmir by providing sturdy and durable materials for the construction of temples. Stone was used for the base, walls, and pillars, while wood was used for the roof and doors. Brick was used for the filling between the stone structures.

Q. no.3 What were the intricate carvings and sculptures used in temple architecture in ancient Kashmir?

Ans. The intricate carvings and sculptures used in temple architecture in ancient Kashmir included depictions of gods and goddesses, mythical creatures, and scenes from

Hindu mythology. These carvings were done with great attention to detail and often had symbolic meanings.

Q. no.4 What was the typical plan of a temple in ancient Kashmir?

Ans. The typical plan of a temple in ancient Kashmir was square or rectangular, with a central hall and a small shrine for the deity. The entrance to the temple was usually through a porch or a mandapa.

Q. no.5 What was the roof style used in temple architecture in ancient Kashmir?

Ans. The roof style used in temple architecture in ancient Kashmir was a pyramidal shape, with a central spire or shikhara. The shikhara was often intricately carved and decorated.

Q. no.6 What was the significance of the central spire in temple architecture in ancient Kashmir?

Ans. The central spire or shikhara in temple architecture in ancient Kashmir was considered to represent the mountain peaks that were believed to be the abode of the gods. It was also believed to be the point where the divine energy of the deity was concentrated.

Q. no.7 What materials were used for decoration in temple architecture in ancient Kashmir?

Ans. The materials used for decoration in temple architecture in ancient Kashmir included stone carvings, wooden panels, stucco work, and frescoes. These decorations were often brightly coloured and depicted scenes from Hindu mythology.

Q. no.8 How did temple architecture in ancient Kashmir influence later temple architecture in India?

Ans. Temple architecture in ancient Kashmir influenced later temple architecture in India by introducing new features such as the use of wood for the roof and intricate stone carvings. The pyramidal roof and central spire were also adopted in many other parts of India.

Medium Answer Type Questions

Q. no.1 What were the key features of temple architecture in ancient Kashmir?

Ans. Temple architecture in ancient Kashmir was characterized by the use of local materials such as limestone and sandstone, intricate stone carvings, delicate stucco work, and an emphasis on symmetry and balance. Temples were typically designed to be grand and impressive, with complex layouts that incorporated courtyards, pavilions, and multiple shrines.

Q. no.2 How did the architecture of Kashmiri temples differ from those in other regions of India?

Ans. Kashmiri temple architecture was distinct from other regions of India in several ways. The use of local materials and innovative construction techniques was a hallmark of the region, as was the incorporation of elements of Persian and Central Asian styles. The region also placed a greater emphasis on ornate roof decorations and intricate stone carvings, which were often combined with delicate stucco work.

Q. no.3 What role did water play in the design of Kashmiri temples?

Ans. Water played an important role in the design of Kashmiri temples, and many temples were built near rivers, lakes, or springs. Water was often used as a decorative element, with elaborate fountains, pools, and channels incorporated into temple courtyards and gardens. The sound of flowing water was also believed to be spiritually purifying and was thought to enhance the overall atmosphere of the temple.

Q. no.4 What is the significance of the Martand Sun Temple in Kashmiri temple architecture?

Ans. Martand Sun Temple is one of the most impressive examples of Kashmiri temple architecture, with a complex layout that emphasises symmetry and balance. The temple features intricate stone carvings, delicate stucco work, and a central courtyard that was surrounded by a series of pavilions and shrines. The temple's innovative use of materials and construction techniques, such as the use of large blocks of limestone, helped to establish Kashmir as a centre of architectural excellence.

Long Answer Type Questions

Q. no.1 What were the prominent features of temple architecture in ancient Kashmir, and how did they contribute to the uniqueness of Kashmiri temples?

Ans. The prominent features of temple architecture in ancient Kashmir were the use of various materials such as stone, wood, and brick, intricate carvings and sculptures, a square or rectangular plan, a pyramidal roof, and a central spire or shikhara. These features contributed to the uniqueness of Kashmiri temples in several ways. Firstly, the use of stone, wood, and brick provided sturdy and durable materials for the construction of temples. Secondly, the intricate carvings and sculptures on the temples depicted gods and goddesses, mythical creatures, and scenes from Hindu mythology, and were done with great attention to detail, making the temples stand out as works of art. Thirdly, the square or rectangular plan with a central hall and small shrine for the deity was a distinctive feature of Kashmiri temples. Fourthly, the pyramidal roof with a central spire or shikhara was also unique to Kashmiri temples and was considered to represent the mountain peaks that were believed to be the abode of the gods. Finally, the decorations on the temples, including stone carvings, wooden panels, stucco work, and frescoes, were often brightly coloured and depict scenes from Hindu mythology, making the temples not only religious centres but also cultural landmarks.

Q. no. 2 How did the temple architecture of ancient Kashmir influence later temple architecture in India, and what were some of the key features that were adopted in other parts of India?

Ans. The temple architecture of ancient Kashmir had a significant influence on later temple architecture in India. One of the key features that were adopted in other parts of India was the use of wood for the roof, which was a distinctive feature of Kashmiri temples. This technique was adopted in other parts of India, such as Rajasthan and Gujarat. Another key feature that was adopted was the pyramidal roof with a central spire or shikhara, which became a hallmark of North Indian temple architecture. The intricate stone carvings on Kashmiri temples were also influential, and later temple architecture in India adopted similar carving techniques to depict scenes from Hindu mythology. Finally, the square or rectangular plan with a central hall and small shrine for the deity, which was a distinctive feature of Kashmiri temples, was also adopted in other parts of India, such as Rajasthan and Gujarat. Overall, the temple architecture of ancient Kashmir had a lasting impact on Indian temple architecture, and its unique features continue to be celebrated and admired by visitors and scholars alike.

Chapter-IV

Short Answer Type Questions

Q. no.1 Where is the Tomb of Zain-ul-Abidin's Mother located?

Ans. The Tomb of Zain-ul-Abidin's Mother is located in Srinagar, Jammu and Kashmir, India.

Q. no.2 Who was Zain-ul-Abidin's Mother?

Ans. Zain-ul-Abidin's mother Miran was a noblewoman of the Shah Miri dynasty of Kashmir who lived during the 15th century.

Q. no.3 What is the architectural style of the Tomb of Zain-ul-Abidin's Mother?

Ans. The architectural style of the Tomb of Zain-ul-Abidin's Mother is a blend of Persian and Islamic styles and is considered an important example of Kashmiri architecture.

Q. no.4 When was the Tomb of Zain-ul-Abidin's Mother built?

Ans. The Tomb of Zain-ul-Abidin's Mother was built in the 15th century, during the reign of Zain-ul-Abidin, who was the eighth Sultan of the Shah Miri dynasty.

Q. no.5 What is the historical significance of the Tomb of Zain-ul-Abidin's Mother?

Ans. The Tomb of Zain-ul-Abidin's Mother is historically significant as it represents the cultural and architectural heritage of the Kashmiri people, and it also reflects the patronage of art and architecture by the rulers of the Shah Miri dynasty.

Q. no.6 Q1: What is Mazar-I-Salateen, and where is it located?

Ans. Mazar-I-Salateen is a graveyard located in Srinagar.

Q. no.7 Whose tomb is located in Mazar-I-Salateen, and what is it commonly known as?

Ans. The tomb of Empress Miran (Jonaraja's Meradevi), the mother of Budshah Zain-Ul-Abidin is located in Mazar-I-Salateen and it is commonly known as Budshah's tomb.

Q. no.8 Where is Budshah's tomb located, and what is the area called?

Ans. Budshah's tomb is located in the fussy lanes of Shahr-e-Khaas near the Old Zaina Kadal area of Srinagar.

Q. no.9 Who was Madin Sahib and where was he originally from?

Ans. Madin Sahib was born Syed Mohammad Madani and lived in Medina.

Q. no. 10 Where is the Tomb of Madin Sahib located?

Ans. The Tomb of Madin Sahib is located to the north of Madin Sahib Mosque in the Zadibal region of Srinagar.

Q. no.11 What is the architectural style of the Tomb of Madin Sahib?

Ans. The Tomb of Madin Sahib is an attractive building built in the 15th-century style of architecture prevalent in Kashmir.

Q. no.12 What is the decoration on the spandrel of the entrance to the Tomb of Madin Sahib?

Ans. At the spandrel of the entrance to the Tomb of Madin Sahib, there is a well-executed representation of half man and half beast in glazed tiles.

Q. no.13 What is the Madin Sahib Mosque and who built it?

Ans. The Madin Sahib Mosque was built by Sultan Zain-ul-Abideen (Budshah) in 1448 for Syed Mohammad Madani and is located close to the Tomb of Madin Sahib.

Medium Answer Type Questions

Q. no.1 Who were the patrons of the Tomb of Zain-ul-Abidin's Mother?

Ans. The Tomb of Zain-ul-Abidin's Mother was built under the patronage of Zain-ul-Abidin, who was the eighth

Sultan of the Shah Miri dynasty of Kashmir. The tomb was built in memory of his mother, who was a noblewoman of the dynasty.

Q. no.2 What is the influence of Persian architecture on the Tomb of Zain-ul-Abidin's Mother?

Ans. The Tomb of Zain-ul-Abidin's Mother shows a strong influence on Persian architecture, which can be seen in its design, such as the use of the rectangular plan and the dome on top of the structure. The intricate carvings and calligraphy on the walls and ceilings of the tomb also reflect the Persian influence on the architecture.

Q. no.3 What is the historical significance of the Tomb of Zain-ul-Abidin's Mother for the Kashmiri people?

Ans. The Tomb of Zain-ul-Abidin's Mother is considered an important cultural and historical site for the Kashmiri people. It reflects the architectural heritage of the region, and it also symbolizes the patronage of art and architecture by the rulers of the Shah Miri dynasty, who played a significant role in shaping the culture and identity of Kashmir.

Q. no.4 What are the similarities and differences between the Madni's Tomb and the Tomb of Zain-ul-Abidin's Mother?

Ans. Both the Madni's Tomb and the Tomb of Zain-ul-Abidin's Mother are examples of Islamic architecture in India, but they differ in their design and features. The Madni's Tomb has a larger central dome, while the Tomb of Zain-ul-Abidin's Mother has a rectangular structure with a smaller dome on top. The Madni's Tomb features intricate carvings and calligraphy on its walls, while the Tomb of Zain-ul-Abidin's Mother has more elaborate carvings and calligraphy. However, both structures represent the cultural and architectural heritage of India and the Islamic world.

Q.no.5 Who were the architects and craftsmen behind the construction of Madni's Tomb and the Tomb of Zain-ul-Abidin's Mother?

Ans. The names of the architects and craftsmen who worked on the construction of Madni's Tomb and the Tomb of Zain-ul-Abidin's Mother are not known. However, it is believed that they were skilled craftsmen from India and Persia who were proficient in the techniques of Islamic architecture.

Q. no.6 What challenges did the architects and craftsmen face while constructing these structures?

Ans. The architects and craftsmen who worked on the construction of these structures faced various challenges, such as the complex design of the structures, the use of heavy building materials, and the harsh weather conditions of the region. They had to use innovative techniques and tools to overcome these challenges and create these magnificent works of Islamic architecture.

Long Answer Type Questions

Q. no.1 How did the political and religious climate of the Sultanate period influence the architecture of Madni's Tomb and the Tomb of Zain-ul-Abidin's Mother?

Ans. During the Sultanate period in India, the political and religious climate played a significant role in shaping the architecture of the period. The rulers of this period were Muslim, and they brought with them the Islamic architectural style that was popular in the Middle East and Central Asia. However, they also incorporated local Indian architectural styles and techniques, which resulted in the development of the Indo-Islamic architectural style.

The Madni's Tomb is an excellent example of this fusion of styles. It features intricate geometric patterns, calligraphy, and lattice work on its walls and ceilings, which are typical of the Islamic architectural style. However, the use of red sandstone, which is indigenous to India, and the large central dome supported by four smaller domes, which is a feature of Indian architecture, reflect the Indian influence on the structure.

Similarly, the Tomb of Zain-ul-Abidin's Mother reflects the influence of the Islamic architectural style, particularly the Persian style. The rectangular plan of the structure and the dome on top of the structure are features of Persian architecture. However, the intricate carvings and calligraphy on the walls and ceilings reflect the Indian influence on the structure.

Q. no.2 What is the historical significance of Madni's Tomb and the Tomb of Zain-ul-Abidin's Mother for the cultural heritage of India?

Ans. The Madni's Tomb and the Tomb of Zain-ul-Abidin's Mother are significant cultural and historical sites in India. These structures reflect the rich architectural heritage of the country and the cultural influence of the

Islamic world on India. They are also a testament to the skill and craftsmanship of the architects and craftsmen of the period.

These structures are not only important as examples of Islamic architecture in India but also for their historical significance. The Madni's Tomb is the tomb of a Sufi saint who played an essential role in spreading the teachings of Islam in India. The Tomb of Zain-ul-Abidin's Mother is a tribute to a noblewoman of the Shah Miri dynasty, who played a significant role in shaping the history of Kashmir.

Moreover, these structures have also influenced the development of later architectural styles in India. The fusion of Indian and Islamic architectural styles seen in these structures contributed to the development of the Indo-Islamic architectural style, which became a hallmark of Mughal architecture in India. Therefore, these structures are an essential part of India's cultural heritage and a testament to the country's rich and diverse history.

Chapter-V

Very Short Answer Type Questions

Q. no.1 What is Mughal architecture?

Ans. Mughal architecture is the style of architecture developed by the Mughals in India during the 16th and 17th centuries.

Q. no. 2 What is Nagar Nagar City?

Ans. Nagar Nagar City is a town in the Indian state of Jammu and Kashmir.

Q. no.3 What is Pathar Masjid?

Ans. Pathar Masjid is a mosque located in the town of Nagar Nagar City.

Q. no.4 What is Jamia Masjid?

Ans. Jamia Masjid is a mosque located in the old city of Nagar Nagar City.

Q. no.5 What is Pari Mahal?

Ans. Pari Mahal is a historic monument located on a hilltop in Nagar Nagar City.

Q. no.6 What are Sarais on Mughal Road?

Ans. Sarais (Inns) on Mughal Road are historic roadside inns built during the Mughal era to provide accommodation for travellers.

Q. no.7 Who were the Mughals?

Ans. The Mughals were a dynasty of Muslim emperors who ruled over India from the early 16th to the mid-19th century.

Q. no.8 What is the significance of Mughal architecture?

Ans. Mughal architecture is known for its grandeur, intricate designs, and use of materials like marble and red sandstone. It has had a significant impact on the architectural styles of India and other countries.

Q. no.9 What is the history of Nagar Nagar City?

Ans. Nagar Nagar City was founded in the 14th century by a local ruler named Raja Udham Singh. It served as an important trading centre on the Silk Route and was later ruled by the Mughals.

Q. no.10 What is unique about Pathar Masjid?

Ans. athar Masjid is unique because it is one of the few mosques in India that is entirely built of stones.

Q. no.11 What is the architecture of Jamia Masjid?

Ans. Jamia Masjid is a fine example of Mughal architecture, with its large courtyard, domes, and minarets.

Q. no.12 What is the story behind the Pari Mahal?

Ans. Pari Mahal was built in the 17th century as a pleasure garden for Mughal Prince Dara Shikoh. It later served as a Buddhist monastery and is now a popular tourist attraction.

Q. no.12 How were the Sarais on Mughal Road used?

Ans. The Sarais on Mughal Road were used as rest houses and inns for travellers, particularly those on the Silk Route. They were also used to store goods and as meeting places for merchants.

Q. no.13 What is the Mughal Road?

Ans. The Mughal Road is an ancient trade route that connects the Jammu region of India with the Kashmir Valley.

Q. no.14 What are some notable features of Mughal architecture?

Ans. Some notable features of Mughal architecture include the use of domes, minarets, arches, intricate floral and geometric patterns, and the use of calligraphy.

Q. no.16 Who were some famous Mughal emperors associated with Mughal architecture?

Ans. Some famous Mughal emperors associated with Mughal architecture include Akbar, Jahangir, Shah Jahan, and Aurangzeb.

Q. no.17 What is the significance of calligraphy in Mughal architecture?

Ans. Calligraphy was an important aspect of Mughal architecture, as it was used to decorate buildings with verses from the Quran and other religious texts.

Q. no.18 What is the current state of preservation of these Mughal buildings and structures?

Ans. Many Mughal buildings and structures have been well-preserved and are major tourist attractions in India. However, some have suffered from neglect and damage over time, and efforts are being made to restore and protect them.

Q. no.19 What materials were commonly used in Mughal architecture?

Ans. Mughal architecture commonly used materials such as red sandstone, marble, and brick.

Q. 20 How did Mughal architecture influence other architectural styles in India?

Ans. Mughal architecture had a significant impact on other architectural styles in India, including Rajput and Sikh architecture. It also influenced architecture in other countries such as Pakistan, Bangladesh, and Afghanistan.

Q. no.21 What is the significance of the Silk Route?

Ans. The Silk Route was an important trade network that connected China with the Mediterranean region, facilitating the exchange of goods, ideas, and cultures between the East and the West.

Q. no.22 How did the Mughals contribute to the development of Indian culture?

Ans. The Mughals made significant contributions to Indian culture, including the promotion of Persian literature, the development of Mughal art, and the patronage of music and dance. They also introduced new architectural styles and techniques to India.

Q. no.23 What is the current state of preservation of the Sarais on Mughal Road?

Ans. The Sarais on Mughal Road has suffered from neglect and damage over time, and many of them are in a state of disrepair. However, efforts are being made to restore and preserve them as important cultural and historical landmarks.

Q. no.24 What is the importance of preserving Mughal architecture and structures?

Ans. Preserving Mughal architecture and structures is important because it helps to maintain India's cultural heritage and history. It also serves as a reminder of the achievements and contributions of the Mughals to Indian society and culture.

Q. no.25 What is the significance of the Mughal Road today?

Ans. The Mughal Road is still an important trade route, connecting the Jammu region of India with the Kashmir

Valley. It is also a popular tourist destination, with many historic landmarks and natural attractions along the way.

Q. no.26 How has Mughal architecture influenced modern architecture in India?

Ans. Mughal architecture has influenced modern architecture in India in many ways, such as the use of arches, domes, and minarets in contemporary buildings. It has also inspired the use of intricate patterns and calligraphy in modern design.

Q. no.27 What is the significance of the Pathar Masjid?

Ans. The Pathar Masjid is a historic mosque in Jammu and Kashmir, India, and is significant for its unique architecture and historical importance.

Q. no.28 What is the significance of the Jamia Masjid in Srinagar?

Ans. The Jamia Masjid in Srinagar is one of the oldest and most important mosques in Kashmir and is significant for its architecture and religious and cultural importance.

Q. no.29 What is the Pari Mahal and its significance?

Ans. The Pari Mahal is a historic monument in Srinagar, Kashmir, and is significant for its unique architecture and historical importance. It is also known for its beautiful gardens and scenic views.

Q. no.30 What is the significance of the Nagar Nagar City in India?

Ans. Nagar Nagar City is a historic town in Rajasthan, India, and is significant for its rich cultural heritage, architecture, and religious importance. It is known for its many temples and other historic landmarks.

Medium Answers Type Questions

Q. no.1 What were some of the most significant innovations in Mughal architecture, and how did they contribute to the development of the style?

Ans. One of the most significant innovations in Mughal architecture was the use of the true arch, which allowed for greater height and stability in buildings. Another important feature was the use of the dome, which created a sense of grandeur and spaciousness in buildings. Mughal architecture also featured intricate floral and geometric patterns, as well as calligraphy, which was used to decorate buildings with verses from the Quran and other religious texts. These innovations helped to create a distinct style of architecture that reflected the values and beliefs of the Mughal dynasty and contributed to the development of a unique Indian architectural style.

Q. no.2 What were some of the factors that contributed to the popularity of Mughal architecture in India, and how did it become an integral part of the country's cultural heritage?

Ans. Mughal architecture became popular in India for some reasons. Firstly, it was associated with the Mughal dynasty, which ruled over much of India for several centuries and was seen as a symbol of the power and prestige of the ruling elite. Secondly, Mughal architecture was admired for its unique style, which combined elements of Persian, Indian, and Central Asian architecture, and reflected the diverse cultural influences that had shaped the Mughal Empire. Finally, Mughal architecture was appreciated for its beauty and elegance and was seen as a way of expressing the values and beliefs of Indian society. Over time, Mughal architecture became an integral part of India's cultural heritage and remains an important influence on contemporary architecture in the country.

Q. no.3 How have efforts to preserve Mughal architecture and structures evolved, and what are some of the challenges that continue to face preservation efforts today?

Ans. Efforts to preserve Mughal architecture and structures have evolved, and have become more systematic and focused in recent years. Governments, cultural organizations, and private individuals have all played a role in preserving these landmarks, through initiatives such as restoration, conservation, and documentation. However, preservation efforts face several challenges, including lack of funding, lack of public awareness and appreciation, and the impact of climate change and natural disasters. Despite these challenges, preservation efforts continue to be an important part of India's cultural heritage and play a vital role in ensuring that these landmarks are protected for future generations to enjoy.

Q. no.4 What is the historical significance of the Mughal Road, and how has it influenced the development of the regions it connects?

Ans. The Mughal Road is a historic trade route that was used by the Mughal emperors to travel between Delhi and

Kashmir. It played an important role in the economic and cultural exchange between the two regions and helped to foster the development of trade, commerce, and cultural exchange. The road also facilitated the spread of Islam in the region, as many of the Mughal emperors were patrons of the religion. Today, the Mughal Road remains an important transport link between the Jammu region and the Kashmir Valley and has influenced the development of the regions it connects by facilitating the movement of people, goods, and ideas.

Q. no.5 How did the Mughals use architecture to legitimize their rule, and what were some of how their architectural style reflected their power and prestige?

Ans. The Mughals used architecture as a means of legitimizing their rule, by building grand monuments and structures that reflected their power and prestige. They commissioned many important buildings, such as forts, palaces, mosques, and tombs that were designed to showcase their wealth and status. The architectural style of the Mughals was characterized by grandeur and elegance that reflected the values of the dynasty, and incorporated elements of Persian, Indian, and Central Asian architecture. The use of intricate floral and geometric patterns, as well as calligraphy, reflected the Mughals' appreciation for art and culture, and their desire to create a distinctive architectural style that would reflect their unique place in Indian history.

Q. no.6 What were some of the key characteristics of Mughal architecture, and how did they differ from other styles of Indian architecture?

Ans. Some of the key characteristics of Mughal architecture include the use of the true arch and the dome, as well as the incorporation of intricate floral and geometric patterns and calligraphy. The style was also characterized by grandeur and elegance that reflected the values of the dynasty and incorporated elements of Persian, Indian, and Central Asian architecture. Mughal architecture differed from other styles of Indian architecture in that it was heavily influenced by the cultures and traditions of the Mughals, who were of Central Asian origin. The style was also characterized by a fusion of different architectural styles and techniques, which created a unique and distinctive form of Indian architecture.

Long Answer Type Questions

Q. no.1 How did Mughal architecture influence the development of Indian architecture, and what are some examples of its lasting impact?

Ans. Mughal architecture had a profound impact on the development of Indian architecture and remains one of the most important influences on the country's architectural heritage. The Mughals brought with them a rich cultural heritage that was reflected in their architecture, which incorporated elements of Persian, Indian, and Central Asian architecture. They commissioned many important buildings, such as forts, palaces, mosques, and tombs that were designed to showcase their wealth and status and reflect their unique place in Indian history.

One of the lasting impacts of Mughal architecture is its use of the true arch, which allowed for greater height and stability in buildings. The use of the dome was another important feature, which created a sense of grandeur and spaciousness in buildings. Mughal architecture also featured intricate floral and geometric patterns, as well as calligraphy, which was used to decorate buildings with verses from the Quran and other religious texts.

Some of the most important examples of Mughal architecture include the Taj Mahal, the Red Fort, and the Jama Masjid. The Taj Mahal is one of the most famous and iconic landmarks in India and is renowned for its elegant white marble dome and intricate calligraphy. The Red Fort, located in Delhi, is an important symbol of the power and prestige of the Mughal dynasty and features impressive ramparts, palaces, and gardens. The Jamia Masjid is one of the largest and most impressive mosques in India and features a massive courtyard, towering minarets, and a beautiful dome.

The influence of Mughal architecture can also be seen in other architectural styles in India, including the Indo-Islamic and Rajput styles. These styles incorporate many of the same features and techniques as Mughal architecture and reflect the lasting impact of the Mughal dynasty on Indian culture and history. Overall, Mughal architecture remains an important part of India's cultural heritage and continues to inspire and influence architects and designers around the world.

Q. no.2 How did the Mughal emperors use architecture to express their religious and cultural beliefs, and what are some examples of the religious and cultural influences in Mughal architecture?

Ans. The Mughal emperors used architecture as a means of expressing their religious and cultural beliefs and incorporated a wide range of religious and cultural influences into their buildings and structures. Islam was a particularly important influence, and the Mughals commissioned many impressive mosques and other Islamic buildings throughout India.

One of the most important examples of Islamic architecture in India is the Jama Masjid, which was built by the Mughal emperor Shah Jahan in Delhi. The mosque features a massive courtyard, towering minarets, and a beautiful dome, and is one of the largest and most impressive mosques in India. The mosque is adorned with intricate floral and geometric patterns, as well as calligraphy from the Quran and other religious texts, which reflect the importance of Islam in Mughal culture.

Another important influence on Mughal architecture was Hinduism, which was the dominant religion in India before the arrival of the Mughals. The Mughals were known for their religious tolerance and incorporated many elements of Hindu architecture into their buildings and structures. The famous Taj Mahal, for example, features many elements of Hindu architecture, including the use of red sandstone and white marble, as well as intricate floral and geometric patterns.

Mughal architecture also incorporated elements of Persian and Central Asian architecture, which reflected the cultural heritage of the Mughal dynasty. Persian architecture was particularly influential, and many of the Mughal buildings feature intricate tile work and other decorative elements that were typical of Persian architecture.

Q. no.3 How did Mughal architecture influence the development of architecture in Kashmir, and what are some examples of Mughal architecture in Kashmir?

Ans. Mughal architecture had a significant impact on the development of architecture in Kashmir, and many important Mughal buildings and structures can still be seen in the region today. The Mughals were known for their architectural and cultural achievements, and they brought with them a rich heritage that was reflected in their buildings and structures.

One of the most important examples of Mughal architecture in Kashmir is Nagar Nagar City, which was founded by the Mughal emperor Jahangir in the early 17th century. The city is located in the heart of the Kashmir Valley and features many impressive buildings and structures, including the Shalimar Bagh, which is a beautiful Mughal garden that is renowned for its fountains, pools, and terraces.

Another important example of Mughal architecture in Kashmir is the Pathar Masjid, which is a beautiful mosque that was built by the Mughal emperor Aurangzeb in the 17th century. The mosque is located in the heart of Srinagar and is known for its elegant white marble facade, as well as its intricate floral and geometric patterns.

The Jamia Masjid in Srinagar is another important example of Mughal architecture in Kashmir. The mosque was built by Sultan Sikandar Shah in the 14th century but was later expanded and renovated by the Mughals in the 17th century. The mosque features a massive courtyard, towering minarets, and a beautiful dome, and is one of the largest and most impressive mosques in the region.

The Pari Mahal, which is a beautiful palace that was built by the Mughal emperor Shah Jahan in the 17th century, is also an important example of Mughal architecture in Kashmir. The palace is located on a hill overlooking Srinagar and is known for its beautiful gardens, as well as its impressive architecture.

Finally, the Sarais on the Mughal Road is an important example of Mughal architecture in Kashmir. The Sarais were built by the Mughals in the 17th century as a way of providing rest and shelter to travellers on the Mughal Road, which was an important trade route that connected Kashmir with the rest of the Mughal Empire. The Sarais are known for their impressive architecture, as well as their beautiful gardens and courtyards.

Q. no.4 What are some unique features of Mughal architecture in Kashmir, and how do they reflect the cultural and religious influences of the Mughals?

Ans. Mughal architecture in Kashmir is characterized by its grandeur, elegance, and sophistication. The Mughals were known for their unique blend of Persian, Indian, and Central Asian architectural styles, which they brought with them to Kashmir. Some of the unique features of Mughal architecture in Kashmir include intricate floral and geometric patterns, elegant arches and domes, and the use of marble and red sandstone in construction.

These features reflect the cultural and religious influences of the Mughals, who were deeply influenced by Islamic and Persian culture. The Mughals were known for their love of gardens and nature, and this is reflected in the many beautiful Mughal gardens that can be seen in Kashmir. These gardens feature fountains, pools, and terraces, and are designed to evoke a sense of harmony and tranquillity.

Another unique feature of Mughal architecture in Kashmir is the use of calligraphy and decorative art. The Mughals were known for their love of literature and poetry, and this is reflected in the intricate calligraphy and decorative art that can be seen on many Mughal buildings and structures in Kashmir.

In addition, the Mughals were known for their tolerance and inclusiveness, and this is reflected in the many examples of syncretic architecture in Kashmir. For example, the Pathar Masjid features both Islamic and Hindu architectural elements, and the Jamia Masjid features a blend of Islamic and Buddhist architectural styles.

Overall, Mughal architecture in Kashmir reflects the rich cultural and religious heritage of the Mughals, as well as their love of beauty, nature, and literature. The unique features of Mughal architecture in Kashmir have had a lasting impact on the region, and continue to inspire architects and artists today.

Q. no.5 How did the Mughal Road and its associated Sarais influence the development of trade and commerce in Kashmir during the Mughal era?

Ans. The Mughal Road was an important trade route that connected Kashmir with the rest of the Mughal Empire and played a significant role in the development of trade and commerce in the region during the Mughal era. The road was built by the Mughals in the 17th century and was used to transport goods and supplies between Kashmir and the rest of the empire.

Along the Mughal Road, the Mughals built several Sarais, which were rest houses that provided shelter and food to travellers. The Sarais were strategically located along the road and played an important role in the development of trade and commerce in the region. They provided a safe and comfortable place for travellers to rest and also served as a hub for trade and commerce.

The Sarais were equipped with a range of facilities, including stables for horses and camels, kitchens for cooking, and courtyards for socializing. This made them an ideal place for traders and merchants to meet, exchange goods, and conduct business. The Sarais also provided employment opportunities for locals, as many people were hired to work in kitchens, stables, and other facilities.

The development of trade and commerce along the Mughal Road had a significant impact on the economy of Kashmir. It allowed for the exchange of goods and ideas between Kashmir and the rest of the Mughal Empire and helped to stimulate economic growth and development in the region. Kashmir became known for its high-quality textiles, carpets, and handicrafts, which were in high demand throughout the empire.

In addition, the Mughals established some markets and bazaars along the Mughal Road, which further facilitated trade and commerce in the region. These markets attracted merchants and traders from all over the empire and helped to establish Kashmir as an important centre of trade and commerce.

Overall, the Mughal Road and its associated Sarais played a critical role in the development of trade and commerce in Kashmir during the Mughal era. They helped to connect Kashmir with the rest of the empire and stimulated economic growth and development in the region.

Q. no.5 What are the notable features of Mughal architecture in Kashmir, and how did the development of the Mughal Road and Sarais contribute to the economic growth and development of the region during the Mughal Empire?

Ans. Mughal architecture in Kashmir is characterized by a unique blend of Persian, Indian, and Central Asian architectural styles, and features intricate floral and geometric patterns, elegant arches and domes, and the use of marble and red sandstone in construction. Mughal gardens, calligraphy, and syncretic architecture are also notable features of Mughal architecture in Kashmir.

The Mughal Road, built in the 17th century, was an important trade route that connected Kashmir with the rest of the Mughal Empire. Along the road, the Mughals built several Sarais, which were rest houses that provided shelter and food to travelers and served as a hub for trade and commerce. The development of trade and commerce along the Mughal Road had a significant impact on the economy of Kashmir, stimulating economic growth and development in the region and establishing it as an important center of trade and commerce.

Chapter-VI

Very Short Answer Type Questions

Q. no.1 What are the Mughal Gardens of Kashmir?

Ans. The Mughal Gardens of Kashmir are a group of historic gardens built during the Mughal era in the Indian state of Jammu and Kashmir.

Q. no.2 What are the names of the Mughal Gardens of Kashmir?

Ans. The names of the Mughal Gardens of Kashmir are Shalimar Bagh, Nishat Bagh, and Naseem Bagh.

Q. no.3 Who built the Mughal Gardens of Kashmir?

Ans. The Mughal Gardens of Kashmir were built by Mughal emperors during their reign in the region.

Q. no.4 When were the Mughal Gardens of Kashmir built?

Ans. The Mughal Gardens of Kashmir were built during the 16th and 17th centuries.

Q. no.5 What is the significance of the Mughal Gardens of Kashmir?

Ans. The Mughal Gardens of Kashmir are significant for their historical, architectural, and cultural importance, and are popular tourist attractions.

Q. no.6 Which Mughal emperor built Shalimar Bagh?

Ans. Shalimar Bagh was built by Mughal Emperor Jahangir in 1619.

Q. no.7 Which Mughal emperor built Nishat Bagh?

Ans. Nishat Bagh was built by Mughal Emperor Asif Jah in 1633.

Q. no.8 What is the layout of Nishat Bagh?

Ans. Nishat Bagh is a terraced garden with twelve levels, each representing a zodiac sign.

Q. no.9 What is the main attraction of Shalimar Bagh?

Ans. The main attraction of Shalimar Bagh is the Shalimar Bagh Pavilion, which is located on the fourth terrace of the garden.

Q. no.10 What is the meaning of the name "Naseem Bagh"?

Ans. The name "Naseem Bagh" means "Breeze Garden" in English.

Q. no.11 Where are the Mughal Gardens of Kashmir located?

Ans. The Mughal Gardens of Kashmir are located on the banks of the Dal Lake in Srinagar, Jammu and Kashmir, India.

Q. no.12 What is the architectural style of the Mughal Gardens of Kashmir?

Ans. The Mughal Gardens of Kashmir are built in the traditional Mughal style of garden design, which is a blend of Islamic, Persian, and Indian architectural styles.

Q. no.13 What are some of the features of Naseem Bagh?

Ans. Naseem Bagh is known for its beautiful water channel, which runs through the garden and is surrounded by trees and flowers.

Q. no.14 What is the significance of the Mughal Gardens of Kashmir in Kashmir's history?

Ans. The Mughal Gardens of Kashmir are an important part of Kashmir's history and culture and are considered to be a symbol of the rich cultural heritage of the region.

Q. no.15 Who was the first Mughal emperor to visit Kashmir and initiate the development of Mughal gardens?

Ans. The first Mughal emperor to visit Kashmir and initiate the development of Mughal gardens was Emperor Akbar in the 16th century.

Q. no.16 What was the reason behind the development of Mughal gardens in Kashmir?

Ans. The Mughal emperors developed gardens in Kashmir as a way to escape the heat of the plains and enjoy the cooler climate of the mountains.

Q. no.17 How did the Mughal gardens of Kashmir evolve?

Ans. The Mughal gardens of Kashmir evolved with each successive emperor adding their touches to the gardens, resulting in a unique blend of Mughal, Persian, and Kashmiri styles.

Q. no.18 What is the significance of the layout and design of Mughal gardens?

Ans. The layout and design of Mughal gardens are significant for their use of symmetry and geometry, as well as their incorporation of water features, pavilions, and other architectural elements.

Q. no.19 How did the Mughal gardens of Kashmir contribute to the development of garden design in India?

Ans. The Mughal gardens of Kashmir contributed significantly to the development of garden design in India, and are considered to be an important part of India's cultural heritage. The Mughal garden style has since been replicated in various parts of India and influenced the development of other garden styles in the country.

Q. no.20 Who was the chief architect responsible for designing the Mughal Gardens of Kashmir?

Ans. The chief architect responsible for designing the Mughal Gardens of Kashmir was Ali Mardan Khan, a

Persian nobleman and architect who served as the governor of Kashmir during the Mughal era.

Q. no.21 Who was the Mughal emperor who commissioned the construction of Shalimar Bagh?

Ans. Shalimar Bagh was commissioned by Mughal Emperor Jahangir in 1619.

Q. no.22 Who was the Mughal emperor who commissioned the construction of Nishat Bagh?

Ans. Nishat Bagh was commissioned by Mughal Emperor Asif Jah in 1633.

Q. no.23 Who were some of the other important people involved in the construction of the Mughal Gardens of Kashmir?

Ans. Some of the other important people involved in the construction of the Mughal Gardens of Kashmir include various Mughal emperors, their courtiers and advisors, and skilled craftsmen and artisans who were brought in from other parts of the Mughal empire.

Q. no.24 How did the architects and craftsmen involved in the construction of the Mughal Gardens of Kashmir influence the design and architecture of the region?

Ans. The architects and craftsmen involved in the construction of the Mughal Gardens of Kashmir brought with them a unique blend of Persian, Islamic, and Indian architectural styles, which influenced the design and architecture of the region for centuries to come. Their work also helped to create a unique cultural fusion that is still evident in the art and architecture of the region today.

Q. no.25 What changes did the later Mughal rulers make to the Mughal Gardens of Kashmir?

Ans. The later Mughal rulers made various changes and additions to the Mughal Gardens of Kashmir, including the addition of new pavilions, fountains, and other architectural features.

Q. no.26 Which Mughal emperor added the Chinar Bagh to the Mughal Gardens of Kashmir?

Ans. The Chinar Bagh was added to the Mughal Gardens of Kashmir by Mughal Emperor Shah Jahan in the 17th century.

Q. no.27 Which Mughal emperor commissioned the construction of the Naseem Bagh?

Ans. The Naseem Bagh was commissioned by Mughal Emperor Aurangzeb in the late 17th century.

Q. no.28 What changes did Aurangzeb make to the Mughal Gardens of Kashmir?

Ans. Aurangzeb made various changes to the Mughal Gardens of Kashmir, including the addition of the Naseem Bagh and the renovation of the other gardens.

Q. no.29 How did the later Mughal rulers contribute to the development of garden design in India through the Mughal Gardens of Kashmir?

Ans. The later Mughal rulers continued to add their touches to the Mughal Gardens of Kashmir, resulting in a unique blend of Mughal, Persian, and Kashmiri styles. Their work also helped to popularize the Mughal garden style throughout India, influencing the development of other garden styles in the country.

Q. no.30 What is Char Chinar?

Ans. Char Chinar is a group of four ancient chinar trees that are situated in the middle of the Dal Lake in Srinagar, Kashmir.

Q. no.31 What is the significance of Char Chinar?

Ans. Char Chinar is significant for its natural beauty and cultural importance. The trees are said to be over 400 years old and are a popular tourist attraction in the region.

Q. no.31 What is the history behind the name Char Chinar?

Ans. The name Char Chinar means "four chinar trees" in Kashmiri. According to legend, the trees were planted by a Sufi saint who is said to have blessed them with mystical powers.

Q. no.32 How did Char Chinar become a part of the Mughal Gardens of Kashmir?

Ans. During the Mughal era, the rulers of Kashmir connected the Char Chinar to the shore of the Dal Lake with a causeway, making it a part of the Mughal Gardens of Kashmir.

Q. no.33 What is the design and layout of Char Chinar?

Ans. Char Chinar is a group of four chinar trees that are situated on a small island in the middle of the Dal Lake. The trees are surrounded by a square-shaped garden, which is accessible via a causeway.

Q. no.34 How does Char Chinar contribute to the cultural heritage of Kashmir?

Ans. Char Chinar is an important part of the cultural heritage of Kashmir and is a symbol of the region's natural beauty and cultural richness. It is also a popular destination for tourists who visit the region.

Q. no. 35 What is the architectural style of Char Chinar?

Ans. The architectural style of Char Chinar is a unique blend of Mughal and Kashmiri styles. The causeway that connects the island to the shore is constructed in a typically Mughal style, while the surrounding garden is designed in a traditional Kashmiri style.

Q. no. 36 How is the architecture of Char Chinar similar to the other Mughal Gardens of Kashmir?

Ans. The architecture of Char Chinar is similar to the other Mughal Gardens of Kashmir in its use of geometric patterns, symmetrical layouts, and the incorporation of water features like fountains and pools.

Q. no. 37 What are some of the unique architectural features of Char Chinar?

Ans. Some of the unique architectural features of Char Chinar include the four ancient chinar trees themselves, the Mughal-style causeway that connects the island to the shore, and the surrounding garden, which is designed in a traditional Kashmiri style.

Q. no. 38 How has the architecture of Char Chinar influenced other architectural styles in the region?

Ans. The unique blend of Mughal and Kashmiri styles seen in the architecture of Char Chinar has influenced the development of other architectural styles in the region, particularly in the design of gardens and other outdoor spaces. The symmetrical layout, geometric patterns, and use of water features have become hallmarks of Kashmiri architecture.

Medium Answer-type questions

Q. no.1 What are the Mughal Gardens of Kashmir?

Ans. The Mughal Gardens of Kashmir are a group of gardens located in the Kashmir Valley, which were built during the Mughal era in India. The three main gardens are Shalimar Bagh, Nishat Bagh, and Naseem Bagh.

Q. no. 2 What is the history of the Mughal Gardens of Kashmir?

Ans. The Mughal Gardens of Kashmir were built during the Mughal era, which lasted from the 16th to the 18th century in India. The gardens were built by the Mughal emperors as a way to showcase their power and wealth, and to provide a place for relaxation and recreation.

Q. no.3 What is the design and layout of the Mughal Gardens of Kashmir?

Ans. The Mughal Gardens of Kashmir are designed in a formal, symmetrical style, with terraced gardens, pavilions, fountains, and pools. The gardens are laid out in a series of rectangular terraces, with the main axis running from north to south.

Q. no.4 What are some of the unique features of the Mughal Gardens of Kashmir?

Ans. Some of the unique features of the Mughal Gardens of Kashmir include the use of water features such as fountains and pools, the symmetrical layout, and the combination of Mughal, Persian, and Kashmiri styles of architecture.

Q. no.5 Who was responsible for the construction of the Mughal Gardens of Kashmir?

Ans. The Mughal Gardens of Kashmir were built by the Mughal emperors, including Jahangir, Shah Jahan, and Aurangzeb. Many of the gardens were commissioned by the emperors and were built by skilled artisans and craftsmen.

Q. no.6 What is the significance of the Mughal Gardens of Kashmir?

Ans. The Mughal Gardens of Kashmir are significant for their historical and cultural importance, as well as for their unique blend of architectural styles. The gardens are also an important tourist attraction in the region.

Q. no.7 What are some of the challenges faced in preserving the Mughal Gardens of Kashmir?

Ans. Some of the challenges faced in preserving the Mughal Gardens of Kashmir include environmental degradation, water pollution, and the threat of urban development. Efforts are being made to preserve and restore the gardens for future generations.

Q. no.8 What is the significance of Shalimar Bagh?

Ans. Shalimar Bagh is one of the most famous Mughal Gardens in Kashmir and was built by Emperor Jahangir in the 17th century. It is significant for its layout, which includes three terraces, and its use of water features like fountains and pools.

Q. no. 9 What is the history behind the construction of Nishat Bagh?

Ans. Nishat Bagh was built by Empress Nur Jahan's brother Asif Khan in the 17th century. It is believed that the garden was built to compete with Shalimar Bagh, which was built by Jahangir.

Q. no. 10 What is the significance of Naseem Bagh?

Ans. Naseem Bagh is a garden located on the outskirts of Srinagar and is significant for its connection to the Sufi saint Sheikh Noor-ud-Din Wali. The garden was built by Emperor Akbar in the 16th century and is believed to have been a retreat for the saint.

Q. no. 11 Who designed the Mughal Gardens of Kashmir?

Ans. The Mughal Gardens of Kashmir were designed by a team of skilled architects, artists, and craftsmen. The designs were influenced by Persian and Central Asian styles, as well as local Kashmiri traditions.

Q. no.12 What is the influence of Persian style in the Mughal Gardens of Kashmir?

Ans. The Persian style is evident in the use of water features like fountains and pools, as well as the use of formal, symmetrical layouts. The use of Persian-style architecture was popular during the Mughal era and can be seen in many of the Mughal Gardens of Kashmir.

Q. no.13 What is the influence of Kashmiri style in the Mughal Gardens of Kashmir?

Ans. The Kashmiri style is evident in the use of local materials like wood and stone, as well as in the use of local flora like chinar trees. The use of Kashmiri-style architecture is also evident in the design of the pavilions and other structures in the gardens.

Q. no.14 What is the significance of the chinar tree in the Mughal Gardens of Kashmir?

Ans. The chinar tree is a local species of tree that is commonly found in the Kashmir Valley. It is significant in the Mughal Gardens of Kashmir for its beauty and its cultural importance, as it is a symbol of Kashmiri identity.

Q. no.15 How has the architecture of the Mughal Gardens of Kashmir influenced other architectural styles in India?

Ans. The architecture of the Mughal Gardens of Kashmir has influenced the development of other architectural styles in India, particularly in the design of gardens and other outdoor spaces. The symmetrical layout, geometric patterns, and use of water features have become hallmarks of Indian architecture.

Long Answers Question Type Questions

Q. no.1 What is the history and cultural significance of the Mughal Gardens of Kashmir?

Ans. The Mughal Gardens of Kashmir, including Shalimar Bagh, Nishat Bagh, and Naseem Bagh, were built during the Mughal era in India. The Mughal emperors were known for their love of gardens and they commissioned many of the most beautiful gardens in India. These gardens were built not only for their aesthetic beauty but also for their cultural and spiritual significance.

The Mughal Gardens of Kashmir were designed to showcase the beauty of nature and the skill of the craftsmen who built them. They feature intricate water channels, fountains, and pools, which create a serene atmosphere and help regulate the temperature in the hot summer months.

The Mughal Gardens of Kashmir also have a deep cultural significance. They represent the fusion of Persian, Central Asian, and local Kashmiri architectural styles, which is reflected in the use of water features, symmetrical layouts, and local materials like wood and stone. The gardens were built to be a reflection of the Mughal emperor's power and wealth, and they served as a symbol of the Mughal dynasty's cultural and artistic achievements.

Today, the Mughal Gardens of Kashmir are a major tourist attraction and a source of pride for the people of Kashmir. They continue to inspire artists, architects, and landscape designers, and they represent a rich cultural legacy that has been passed down through the generations.

Q. no.2 How did the architecture of the Mughal Gardens of Kashmir influence other architectural styles in India?

Ans. The architecture of the Mughal Gardens of Kashmir had a significant impact on the development of other architectural styles in India. The symmetrical layouts, geometric patterns, and use of water features in the Mughal Gardens of Kashmir became hallmarks of Indian architecture, particularly in the design of gardens and other outdoor spaces.

The Mughal Gardens of Kashmir were designed by a team of skilled architects, artists, and craftsmen who were influenced by Persian and Central Asian styles, as well as local Kashmiri traditions. The use of water features, including fountains and pools, is a key feature of Persian-style gardens, which were popular during the Mughal era.

The use of local materials, such as wood and stone, is another characteristic of the Mughal Gardens of Kashmir that has influenced other architectural styles in India. The use of local flora, such as the chinar tree, is also significant and reflects the Mughals' respect for the natural beauty of the region.

The symmetrical layout of the gardens, with its geometric patterns and axial symmetry, became a hallmark of Indian architecture, particularly in the design of Mughal-style buildings like the Taj Mahal. The Mughal Gardens of Kashmir also inspired the development of other types of gardens in India, including the pleasure gardens and formal gardens that were popular during the Raj era.

In summary, the architecture of the Mughal Gardens of Kashmir has had a lasting impact on Indian architecture and continues to inspire artists and designers to this day. The fusion of Persian, Central Asian, and local Kashmiri architectural styles has created a unique and enduring legacy that is a testament to the creativity and skill of the craftsmen who built these magnificent gardens.

Q. no.3 What is the history and significance of Chashme Shahi, and what are some of its notable features?

Ans. Chashme Shahi, also known as the Royal Spring Garden, is one of the most famous Mughal Gardens of Kashmir. It was built by the Mughal emperor Shah Jahan in 1632 AD and is located near the famous Dal Lake in Srinagar. The garden is renowned for its natural spring, which is the source of its name, and its stunning architecture and landscape design.

The garden was built during the Mughal era and reflects the Mughals' love for nature and their passion for beauty and elegance. The garden is built on three terraces, each of which is filled with lush greenery, water channels, and fountains. The garden's natural spring feeds into a small pool at the centre of the garden, which is surrounded by a pavilion with a beautiful fountain.

Chashme Shahi is known for its architectural features, which include the use of local materials such as wood and stone, as well as intricate water channels and fountains. The garden's water features are particularly notable, with water flowing through the garden in a series of cascades and pools, creating a peaceful and serene atmosphere. The garden's pathways and walkways are also designed to offer visitors a sense of peace and tranquillity, with shaded areas and cool breezes that offer respite from the heat of the sun.

In addition to its stunning architecture and landscape design, Chashme Shahi is also significant for its cultural and historical importance. The garden has been a site of inspiration for poets and artists for centuries, and it is said that the Mughal emperor Shah Jahan used to visit the garden frequently for its beauty and tranquillity.

Today, Chashme Shahi remains one of the most popular tourist attractions in Kashmir, and it continues to inspire artists, architects, and landscape designers. It is a testament to the creativity and skill of the Mughal craftsmen who built it, and it serves as a reminder of the rich cultural legacy of the region.

Q. no.4 How did the Mughal gardens of Kashmir develop over time, and what are some of their distinctive features?

Ans. The Mughal gardens of Kashmir are renowned for their stunning beauty, exquisite design, and rich history. They were built by the Mughal emperors during the 16th and 17th centuries and were inspired by the Persian concept of paradise gardens. The gardens were designed to reflect the Mughal's love for nature, their passion for beauty, and their desire to create a peaceful and harmonious space.

The earliest Mughal garden in Kashmir was the Bagh-e-Safa, which was built in the early 16th century by the founder of the Mughal dynasty, Babur. However, it was during the reign of Jahangir, the fourth Mughal emperor, that the Mughal gardens of Kashmir reached their zenith. Jahangir was a lover of beauty and the arts, and he was particularly drawn to the natural beauty of Kashmir. He ordered the construction of several magnificent gardens in the region, including the Shalimar, Nishat, and Chashme Shahi gardens.

The Mughal gardens of Kashmir are known for their distinctive features, which include the use of terraces, water channels, fountains, pavilions, and geometric designs. The gardens were designed to provide a sense of tranquillity and harmony, with carefully placed water features and greenery creating a soothing atmosphere. The gardens were also designed to provide respite from the heat of the sun, with shaded areas and cool breezes offering relief from the heat.

One of the most distinctive features of the Mughal gardens of Kashmir is their use of water. Water plays a central role in the gardens, with natural springs and streams feeding into a complex system of water channels, pools, and fountains. The water channels were carefully designed to create a sense of movement and flow, with the sound of water adding to the tranquil atmosphere of the gardens.

Another distinctive feature of the Mughal gardens of Kashmir is their use of pavilions and other architectural features. The gardens feature a range of pavilions, including octagonal and hexagonal pavilions, as well as open-air platforms and terraces. These structures were designed to provide visitors with a place to rest, relax, and enjoy the views of the garden.

Over time, the Mughal gardens of Kashmir continued to evolve and develop, with each successive emperor adding their unique touches and designs. Today, these gardens remain a testament to the creativity and skill of the Mughal craftsmen who built them, and they continue to inspire architects, landscape designers, and nature lovers around the world.

Q. no. 4 What is the significance of Mughal gardens in Kashmir, both historically and culturally?

Ans. The Mughal gardens of Kashmir hold immense historical and cultural significance, not just for the region but also for the wider world. These gardens are a testament to the creativity and ingenuity of the Mughal craftsmen, and they continue to inspire artists, architects, and landscape designers to this day.

Historically, the Mughal gardens of Kashmir are significant because they were built during the height of the Mughal Empire, a period of great cultural and artistic achievement. The gardens were a reflection of the Mughal's love of beauty and their appreciation of nature, and they were designed to provide a place of respite from the hustle and bustle of city life. The gardens were also a symbol of the Mughal's power and wealth, with their magnificent structures and intricate designs reflecting the empire's prestige and influence.

Culturally, the Mughal gardens of Kashmir are significant because they represent a fusion of Persian, Indian, and Central Asian influences. The gardens were built by Mughal emperors who came from diverse cultural backgrounds, and they incorporated elements of each of these cultures into their designs. The gardens also served as a meeting point for scholars, artists, and intellectuals from across the empire, who came together to exchange ideas and share their knowledge.

The gardens of Kashmir are also significant for their impact on the wider world. The Mughals were great patrons of the arts, and their gardens had a profound influence on the development of landscape design and architecture across the globe. The Mughal's use of water, terraces, pavilions, and geometric designs have inspired countless gardens and parks around the world, from the Taj Mahal in India to the Alhambra in Spain.

Today, the Mughal gardens of Kashmir remain an important cultural and historical landmark, attracting visitors from across the globe who come to marvel at their beauty and learn about their rich history. The gardens are a reminder of the Mughal's enduring legacy and their contributions to the world of art, architecture, and landscape design.

Q. no.5 What is the significance of Bagh-e-Safa in the development of Mughal gardens in Kashmir and across the empire?

Ans. Bagh-e-Safa was the earliest Mughal garden in Kashmir, built in the early 16th century by Babur, the founder of the Mughal dynasty. The legacy of this garden is significant, as it laid the foundation for the development of Mughal gardens in Kashmir and across the empire.

Bagh-e-Safa was known for its simple and elegant design, with its focus on symmetry and balance. The garden was divided into four quadrants, each containing a water channel, and was surrounded by a high wall to protect it from the harsh weather of Kashmir.

The garden was not only a place of beauty but also served practical purposes. It was used for growing fruits and vegetables, and it also provided a place for Babur and his followers to relax and escape the stresses of politics and warfare.

The legacy of Bagh-e-Safa can be seen in the development of Mughal gardens throughout the empire. The Mughal emperors who followed Babur, such as Jahangir and Shah Jahan, continued to build gardens in Kashmir and elsewhere in the empire, incorporating elements of Persian, Indian, and Central Asian design.

The Mughal gardens of Kashmir, such as Shalimar, Nishat, and Chashmi Shahi, all owe their origins to the Bagh-e-Safa. The garden also inspired the development of other notable Mughal gardens, such as the famous Taj Mahal complex in Agra.

Today, the legacy of Bagh-e-Safa can still be seen in the gardens and parks that exist throughout the world. Its emphasis on symmetry, balance, and natural beauty continues to inspire landscape designers and architects, who seek to create harmonious and peaceful spaces for people to enjoy.

Q. no.6 How did Mughal gardens influence landscape design and architecture?

Ans. Mughal gardens have had a profound influence on landscape design and architecture, both in the region of South Asia and around the world. These gardens were built during the height of the Mughal Empire and reflect the unique blend of Persian, Indian, and Central Asian influences that characterized the empire's cultural and artistic achievements.

One of the most distinctive features of Mughal gardens is their use of water. The Mughals were expert engineers and they used water to create a variety of effects in their gardens. They built water channels, pools, and fountains, and used them to reflect light and create a sense of movement and tranquillity. The use of water in Mughal gardens has had a lasting impact on landscape design, and it can be seen in many gardens and parks around the world, including the famous Versailles gardens in France.

Another hallmark of Mughal gardens is their use of terraces. The Mughals built gardens on a series of terraces, which allowed them to create different levels and perspectives within the garden. The use of terraces in Mughal gardens has influenced the development of landscape design and architecture, particularly in the creation of public spaces such as plazas and parks.

Mughal gardens are also known for their pavilions and other structures, which were built to provide shade and shelter from the hot sun. These structures were often intricately designed, with ornate carvings and delicate lattice work. The pavilions and other structures in Mughal gardens have had a significant impact on architecture, inspiring the development of buildings such as mosques, tombs, and palaces.

Finally, Mughal gardens are characterized by their use of geometric designs. The gardens were often laid out in a symmetrical pattern, with a central axis that provided a sense of order and balance. This emphasis on geometry and symmetry has influenced landscape design and architecture, particularly in the creation of formal gardens and public spaces.

In conclusion, Mughal gardens have had a profound impact on landscape design and architecture. Their use of water, terraces, pavilions, and geometric designs has influenced the development of gardens and parks around the world, as well as the design of buildings such as mosques, tombs, and palaces. The Mughal's love of beauty and their appreciation of nature continues to inspire artists, architects, and landscape designers to this day.

Q. no.7 What is the symbolism and significance of Mughal gardens?

Ans. Mughal gardens were not simply designed for aesthetic pleasure but also held deep symbolic and cultural significance. They were designed to reflect the Mughals' appreciation of nature, their religious and cultural beliefs, and their social status.

One of the primary symbols in Mughal gardens is water. Water symbolizes purity and life-giving properties in many cultures, and the Mughals were no exception. The extensive use of water channels, pools, and fountains in

Mughal gardens not only provided a sense of tranquillity and coolness but also represented the Mughals' belief in the importance of water as a life-giving force.

Another significant symbol in Mughal gardens is the use of symmetry and geometry. The symmetrical designs of the gardens, with a central axis and terraced levels, represented order and balance. This symbolism reflected the Mughals' belief in the importance of balance and harmony in nature and their society.

Mughal gardens also often incorporated features such as pavilions and other structures. These structures provided shelter from the hot sun and rain, but they also symbolized the Mughals' social status and their appreciation of the finer things in life. The intricately designed structures, with ornate carvings and lattice work, represented the wealth and power of the Mughal Empire.

Finally, Mughal gardens were often designed with specific themes and motifs. For example, the Shalimar Bagh in Kashmir was designed to represent the Mughals' love of beauty, while the Nishat Bagh was designed to symbolize the seven levels of paradise in Islam. These themes and motifs not only added to the beauty and visual interest of the gardens but also reflected the Mughals' religious and cultural beliefs.

In conclusion, Mughal gardens were not just beautiful spaces, but also held deep symbolic and cultural significance. The extensive use of water, symmetrical designs, ornate structures, and thematic motifs all represented the Mughals' appreciation of nature, their religious and cultural beliefs, and their social status. The legacy of Mughal gardens continues to influence landscape design and architecture around the world, and their symbolism and significance remain important today.

Q. no.8 What is the history and significance of the Dara Shikoh Garden?

Ans. The Dara Shikoh Garden, also known as the Shalimar Bagh in Lahore, was built in the mid-17th century by the Mughal prince Dara Shikoh. Dara Shikoh was the eldest son of Emperor Shah Jahan and was known for his interest in Sufi philosophy, art, and literature. He commissioned the garden as a place for contemplation and reflection, as well as for entertaining guests.

The garden was designed in the typical Mughal style, with a central water channel, terraced levels, and ornate pavilions. The garden was also renowned for its extensive use of fountains and water features, which added to the beauty and tranquillity of the space.

However, the garden's significance goes beyond its aesthetic appeal. Dara Shikoh was a patron of the arts and literature, and he often invited scholars and intellectuals to the garden for discussions and debates. The garden became a centre for intellectual and cultural exchange, where ideas were exchanged and new works of literature and art were created.

Unfortunately, Dara Shikoh's life was cut short by his younger brother Aurangzeb, who had him executed in 1659 in a power struggle for the Mughal throne. After Dara Shikoh's death, the garden fell into disrepair and was neglected for many years.

It was only in the late 19th century that the garden was restored and revived by the British colonial authorities. The garden was renovated and some of its original features, such as the water channels and fountains, were restored. Today, the Dara Shikoh Garden is a popular tourist attraction and a reminder of the rich cultural heritage of the Mughal Empire.

In conclusion, the Dara Shikoh Garden is not only a beautiful Mughal garden but also a symbol of intellectual and cultural exchange during the Mughal era. It was built by the Mughal prince Dara Shikoh as a place for contemplation and reflection, as well as for entertaining guests. Its extensive use of water features and ornate pavilions add to its aesthetic appeal, while its history and significance make it an important cultural heritage site.

Chapter-VII

Short Answer Type Questions

Q. no.1 Where is Parihaspora located?

Ans. Parihaspora is located in the Budgam district of Jammu and Kashmir, India.

Q. no.2 What is the significance of Parihaspora?

Ans. Parihaspora was an ancient capital city of Kashmir and is known for its archaeological site that dates back to the 8th century.

Q. no.3 What is the architectural style of the Martand Temple?

Ans. The Martand Temple is an example of Kashmiri architecture, which is a blend of Indian, Persian, and Central Asian styles.

Q. no. 5 Where is the Martand Temple located?

Ans. The Martand Temple is located in the Anantnag district of Jammu and Kashmir, India.

Q. no.6 What is the current condition of the Martand Temple?

Ans. The Martand Temple is in ruins, but the remains of its grand architecture and intricate carvings continue to attract visitors and scholars.

Q. no.7 Who built the Martand Temple?

Ans. The Martand Temple was built by King Lalitaditya Muktapida in the 8th century.

Q. no.8 What is the main deity of the Martand Temple?

Ans. The Martand Temple is dedicated to the Hindu deity Surya, the Sun God.

Q. no.9 What are some of the unique architectural features of the Martand Temple?

Ans. The Martand Temple has 84 columns and is surrounded by a courtyard with a colonnade of 224 columns, making it one of the largest temple complexes in India.

Q. no.10 What is the historical significance of the Parihaspora?

Ans. Parihaspora was an important centre of learning and culture during the rule of the Karkota dynasty in Kashmir and was home to several temples, universities, and libraries.

Q. no.11 What is the current state of preservation of the Parihaspora?

Ans. The Parihaspora archaeological site is under the supervision of the Archaeological Survey of India, and ongoing efforts are being made to preserve and protect the ancient structures and artefacts found there.

Q. no.12 What is the current state of the Martand Temple?

Ans. The Martand Temple is in ruins, and only a small portion of the original structure remains.

Q. no.13 What is the architectural style of the Parihaspora temples?

Ans. The Parihaspora temples are built in the classical Kashmiri style, which is a unique blend of Indian, Persian, and Central Asian architectural styles.

Q. no.14 What is the significance of the Martand Temple in Kashmiri culture?

Ans. The Martand Temple is an important cultural and religious site in Kashmir, and its ruins are a popular tourist destination.

Q. no.15 What is the current state of preservation of the Parihaspora temples?

Ans. The Parihaspora temples are in a state of disrepair, and efforts are being made to restore and preserve the remaining structures.

Medium Answer Type Questions

Q. no.1 What is the historical significance of the Parihaspora in Kashmiri history?

Ans. Parihaspora was the ancient capital of Kashmir during the reign of King Lalitaditya in the 8th century CE.

The city was a hub of learning and culture and was known for its great university, which attracted scholars and students from all over India and Central Asia. Parihaspora was also an important centre of Buddhism and Hinduism, and many temples and monasteries were built in the city during this period.

Q. no.2 What is the architectural significance of the Martand Temple in Kashmiri history?

Ans. The Martand Temple is one of the most significant examples of classical Kashmiri temple architecture. The temple was built in the 8th century CE during the reign of King Lalitaditya and is famous for its elegant and intricate design. The temple is built on a raised platform and features a central hall with a raised platform for the main deity, surrounded by smaller shrines and chambers. The temple is also known for its impressive use of sculptural and decorative elements, including intricate carvings, friezes, and panels.

Q. no.3 What are the challenges faced in preserving the Martand Temple?

Ans. The Martand Temple is in a state of ruins and faces several challenges in terms of preservation and restoration. The temple has suffered significant damage over the years due to natural disasters, neglect, and human-made threats. Additionally, there are several disputes over ownership and management of the site, which have made conservation efforts more difficult. Nevertheless, several restoration projects have been undertaken to preserve the remaining structures and prevent further damage.

Q. no.4 What are the unique features of the Parihaspora temples?

Ans. The Parihaspora temples are built in the classical Kashmiri style, which is a unique blend of Indian, Persian, and Central Asian architectural styles. The temples are known for their impressive use of structural and decorative elements, including intricate carvings, friezes, and ornamental features. The temples are also notable for their use of local building materials, including limestone, sandstone, and brick.

Q. no.5 What is the cultural significance of the Martand Temple in Kashmiri society?

Ans. The Martand Temple is an important cultural and religious site in Kashmir, and its ruins are a popular destination for tourists and pilgrims. The temple is also a symbol of Kashmiri culture and heritage and serves as a reminder of the rich architectural and artistic traditions of the region. Additionally, the temple plays a significant role in the cultural identity and tourism economy of the region.

Long Answer Type Questions

Q. no.1 Can you describe the architectural features and historical significance of the Parihaspora Temple?

Ans. Parihaspora Temple is an ancient temple located in the Parihaspora village of Kashmir. The temple is believed to have been built during the reign of the Karkota dynasty, around the 8th century AD. The temple is constructed of stone and features a rectangular base with four entrances.

The temple also has a shikhara or tower, which is now in ruins.

The temple is significant because it is believed to have been the site of a major religious conference during the reign of Lalitaditya, a prominent ruler of the Karkota dynasty. The conference brought together scholars and theologians from across India to discuss and debate the doctrines of Buddhism, Hinduism, and Jainism. The conference is considered to be one of the most important events in the religious history of Kashmir.

Q. no.2 What are the architectural features and historical significance of Martand Temple?

Ans. Martand Temple, also known as the Sun Temple, is an ancient temple located in the Anantnag district of Kashmir. The temple was built by King Lalitaditya in the 8th century AD and is dedicated to the Hindu god Surya, the sun god. The temple is constructed of stone and features a central shrine with several smaller shrines around it.

The temple is significant because it represents a unique blend of Hindu and Buddhist architectural styles. The temple also features intricate stone carvings, which depict various mythological and religious scenes. The temple is also significant because it was one of the largest and most important temples in Kashmir during the reign of the Karkota dynasty. The temple was destroyed by Sikandar Butshikan, a Muslim ruler, in the 15th century, but its ruins still stand as a testament to the rich cultural heritage of Kashmir.

Chapter-VIII

Short Answer Type Questions

Q. no.1 Where is Parihaspora located?

Ans. Parihaspora is located in the Budgam district of Jammu and Kashmir, India.

Q. no.2 What is the significance of Parihaspora?

Ans. Parihaspora was an ancient capital city of Kashmir and is known for its archaeological site that dates back to the 8th century.

Q. no.3 What is the architectural style of the Martand Temple?

Ans. The Martand Temple is an example of Kashmiri architecture, which is a blend of Indian, Persian, and Central Asian styles.

Q. no. 5 Where is the Martand Temple located?

Ans. The Martand Temple is located in the Anantnag district of Jammu and Kashmir, India.

Q. no.6 What is the current condition of the Martand Temple?

Ans. The Martand Temple is in ruins, but the remains of its grand architecture and intricate carvings continue to attract visitors and scholars.

Q. no.7 Who built the Martand Temple?

Ans. The Martand Temple was built by King Lalitaditya Muktapida in the 8th century.

Q. no.8 What is the main deity of the Martand Temple?

Ans. The Martand Temple is dedicated to the Hindu deity Surya, the Sun God.

Q. no.9 What are some of the unique architectural features of the Martand Temple?

Ans. The Martand Temple has 84 columns and is surrounded by a courtyard with a colonnade of 224 columns, making it one of the largest temple complexes in India.

Q. no.10 What is the historical significance of the Parihaspora?

Ans. Parihaspora was an important centre of learning and culture during the rule of the Karkota dynasty in Kashmir and was home to several temples, universities, and libraries.

Q. no.11 What is the current state of preservation of the Parihaspora?

Ans. The Parihaspora archaeological site is under the supervision of the Archaeological Survey of India, and ongoing efforts are being made to preserve and protect the ancient structures and artefacts found there.

Q. no.12 What is the current state of the Martand Temple?

Ans. The Martand Temple is in ruins, and only a small portion of the original structure remains.

Q. no.13 What is the architectural style of the Parihaspora temples?

Ans. The Parihaspora temples are built in the classical Kashmiri style, which is a unique blend of Indian, Persian, and Central Asian architectural styles.

Q. no.14 What is the significance of the Martand Temple in Kashmiri culture?

Ans. The Martand Temple is an important cultural and religious site in Kashmir, and its ruins are a popular tourist destination.

Q. no.15 What is the current state of preservation of the Parihaspora temples?

Ans. The Parihaspora temples are in a state of disrepair, and efforts are being made to restore and preserve the remaining structures.

Medium Answer Type Questions

Q. no.1 What is the historical significance of the Parihaspora in Kashmiri history?

Ans. Parihaspora was the ancient capital of Kashmir during the reign of King Lalitaditya in the 8th century CE.

The city was a hub of learning and culture and was known for its great university, which attracted scholars and students from all over India and Central Asia. Parihaspora was also an important centre of Buddhism and Hinduism, and many temples and monasteries were built in the city during this period.

Q. no.2 What is the architectural significance of the Martand Temple in Kashmiri history?

Ans. The Martand Temple is one of the most significant examples of classical Kashmiri temple architecture. The temple was built in the 8th century CE during the reign of King Lalitaditya and is famous for its elegant and intricate design. The temple is built on a raised platform and features a central hall with a raised platform for the main deity, surrounded by smaller shrines and chambers. The temple is also known for its impressive use of sculptural and decorative elements, including intricate carvings, friezes, and panels.

Q. no.3 What are the challenges faced in preserving the Martand Temple?

Ans. The Martand Temple is in a state of ruins and faces several challenges in terms of preservation and restoration. The temple has suffered significant damage over the years due to natural disasters, neglect, and human-made threats. Additionally, there are several disputes over ownership and management of the site, which have made conservation efforts more difficult. Nevertheless, several restoration projects have been undertaken to preserve the remaining structures and prevent further damage.

Q. no.4 What are the unique features of the Parihaspora temples?

Ans. The Parihaspora temples are built in the classical Kashmiri style, which is a unique blend of Indian, Persian, and Central Asian architectural styles. The temples are known for their impressive use of structural and decorative elements, including intricate carvings, friezes, and ornamental features. The temples are also notable for their use of local building materials, including limestone, sandstone, and brick.

Q. no.5 What is the cultural significance of the Martand Temple in Kashmiri society?

Ans. The Martand Temple is an important cultural and religious site in Kashmir, and its ruins are a popular destination for tourists and pilgrims. The temple is also a symbol of Kashmiri culture and heritage and serves as a reminder of the rich architectural and artistic traditions of the region. Additionally, the temple plays a significant role in the cultural identity and tourism economy of the region.

Long Answer Type Questions

Q. no.1 Can you describe the architectural features and historical significance of the Parihaspora Temple?

Ans. Parihaspora Temple is an ancient temple located in the Parihaspora village of Kashmir. The temple is believed to have been built during the reign of the Karkota dynasty, around the 8th century AD. The temple is constructed of stone and features a rectangular base with four entrances.

The temple also has a shikhara or tower, which is now in ruins.

The temple is significant because it is believed to have been the site of a major religious conference during the reign of Lalitaditya, a prominent ruler of the Karkota dynasty. The conference brought together scholars and theologians from across India to discuss and debate the doctrines of Buddhism, Hinduism, and Jainism. The conference is considered to be one of the most important events in the religious history of Kashmir.

Q. no.2 What are the architectural features and historical significance of Martand Temple?

Ans. Martand Temple, also known as the Sun Temple, is an ancient temple located in the Anantnag district of Kashmir. The temple was built by King Lalitaditya in the 8th century AD and is dedicated to the Hindu god Surya, the sun god. The temple is constructed of stone and features a central shrine with several smaller shrines around it.

The temple is significant because it represents a unique blend of Hindu and Buddhist architectural styles. The temple also features intricate stone carvings, which depict various mythological and religious scenes. The temple is also significant because it was one of the largest and most important temples in Kashmir during the reign of the Karkota dynasty. The temple was destroyed by Sikandar Butshikan, a Muslim ruler, in the 15th century, but its ruins still stand as a testament to the rich cultural heritage of Kashmir.

Chapter-IX

Very Short Answer Type Questions

Q. no.1 What is Nagar Nagar city?

Ans. Nagar Nagar city is a city in Kashmir.

Q. no.2 What are Mughal Gardens?

Ans. Mughal Gardens are a collection of gardens located in different parts of the Subcontinent.

Q. no.3 What can visitors see in Nagar Nagar city?

Ans. Visitors can see Jamai Masjid, Mughal Gardens, and other attractions in Nagar Nagar city.

Q. no.4 Where is Nagar Nagar city located?

Ans. Nagar Nagar city is located in Kashmir.

Q. no.5 What is Jamaia Masjid?

Ans. Jamaia Masjid is a historic mosque located in Nagar Nagar city.

Q. no.6 What are the Mughal Gardens of Kashmir?

Ans. The Mughal Gardens of Kashmir are a group of gardens built by Mughal emperors, including Shalimar Bagh, Nishat Bagh, and Chashme Shahi.

Q. no.7 Are the Mughal Gardens of Kashmir well-known tourist attractions?

Ans. Yes, the Mughal Gardens of Kashmir are well-known tourist attractions and are visited by thousands of tourists every year.

Q. no.8 What can visitors expect to see at the Mughal Gardens of Kashmir?

Ans. Visitors can expect to see beautifully manicured gardens, fountains, water channels, and other architectural features at the Mughal Gardens of Kashmir.

Q. no.9 What is the best time to visit Nagar Nagar city and the Mughal Gardens of Kashmir?

Ans. The best time to visit Nagar Nagar city and the Mughal Gardens of Kashmir is during the spring and summer months, from March to October.

Q. no.10 What is the history of Jamaia Masjid in Nagar Nagar city?

Ans. Jamaia Masjid was built in the 15th century by Sultan Sikander Shah, and it has been a significant religious and cultural centre in the region ever since.

Q. no.11 Are there any other popular tourist attractions in Nagar Nagar city?

Ans. Yes, some other popular tourist attractions in Nagar Nagar city include Shankaracharya Hill, Pari Mahal, and Dal Lake.

Q. no.12 How long does it take to explore the Mughal Gardens of Kashmir?

Ans. The time it takes to explore the Mughal Gardens of Kashmir depends on the individual's pace, but visitors can typically spend a few hours exploring the gardens.

Q. no.13 What is the history of Nagar Nagar city?

Ans. Nagar Nagar city has a rich history that dates back to ancient times, and it has been ruled by various dynasties throughout history, including the Mughals and the Sikhs.

Q. no.14 What is the significance of Jamaia Masjid in Nagar Nagar city's history?

Ans. Jamia Masjid has played an important role in the religious and cultural history of Nagar Nagar city, and it is considered one of the region's most significant landmarks.

Q. no.15 Who built the Mughal Gardens of Kashmir, and why?

Ans. The Mughal Gardens of Kashmir were built by Mughal emperors, including Jahangir and Shah Jahan, as a way to showcase their power and wealth, and as a means of enjoying the natural beauty of the region.

Q. no.16 How have the Mughal Gardens of Kashmir influenced the region's history and culture?

Ans. The Mughal Gardens of Kashmir have had a significant impact on the region's history and culture, and they are considered a testament to the Mughal's love for nature and art.

Q. no.17 What is the historical significance of the Mughal Gardens of Kashmir's architecture and design?

Ans. The architecture and design of the Mughal Gardens of Kashmir are considered some of the most exquisite in the world, and they represent a fusion of Mughal, Persian, and Islamic styles that have influenced garden design throughout the world.

Q. no.18 Who founded Nagar Nagar city, and when?

Ans. Nagar Nagar city was founded in the 6th century by the Hindu king, Lalitaditya.

Q. no. 19 Who were the Mughal emperors that built the Mughal Gardens of Kashmir?

Ans. The Mughal emperors who built the Mughal Gardens of Kashmir were Jahangir, Shah Jahan, and Aurangzeb.

Q. no. 20 What was the role of Jahangir in the creation of the Mughal Gardens of Kashmir?

Ans. Jahangir was a great lover of nature and gardens, and he is credited with laying the foundation for the Mughal Gardens of Kashmir. He was involved in the design and construction of several gardens, including Shalimar Bagh and Nishat Bagh.

Q. no. 22 What was the role of Nur Jahan in the creation of the Mughal Gardens of Kashmir?

Ans. Nur Jahan, the wife of Jahangir, was a great patron of the arts and architecture, and she is credited with contributing to the design of the Mughal Gardens of Kashmir. She was particularly interested in the design of the water features in the gardens.

Q. no. 23 Who designed the Chashme Shahi garden in the Mughal Gardens of Kashmir?

Ans. The Chashme Shahi garden was designed by Ali Mardan Khan, a Persian nobleman and architect who served in the court of the Mughal emperor Shah Jahan.

Q. no.24 What is the architectural style of Jamaia Masjid in Nagar Nagar city?

Ans. Jamia Masjid in Nagar Nagar city is an excellent example of Indo-Islamic architecture, which combines Hindu and Islamic elements. The mosque features a large courtyard and four minarets.

Q. no. 25 What is the architectural style of the Mughal Gardens of Kashmir?

Ans. The Mughal Gardens of Kashmir feature a blend of Persian and Mughal architectural styles. The gardens are designed to incorporate natural elements, such as water features and the surrounding mountains, into the overall design.

Q. no. 26 What are some of the notable architectural features of the Mughal Gardens of Kashmir?

Ans. Some of the notable architectural features of the Mughal Gardens of Kashmir include the use of symmetry and balance, the use of water channels and fountains, and the incorporation of different levels and terraces into the garden design.

Q. no. 27 Who was responsible for the design of the Mughal Gardens of Kashmir?

Ans. The Mughal Gardens of Kashmir were designed by a team of architects and landscape designers, including Ali Mardan Khan and Nur Jahan.

Q. no.28 What is the significance of the architecture of the Mughal Gardens of Kashmir in garden design history?

Ans. The architecture of the Mughal Gardens of Kashmir is significant in garden design history as it represents a fusion of different architectural styles and has influenced garden design throughout the world.

Q. no.29 What is the significance of Nagar Nagar city in the history of Kashmir?

Ans. Nagar Nagar city is a significant historical and cultural centre in Kashmir, with a rich history that dates back to ancient times. The city has been ruled by various dynasties throughout history and is home to several important landmarks, including Jamaia Masjid.

Q. no. 30 What is the significance of Jamaia Masjid in the history of Kashmir?

Ans. Jamaia Masjid in Nagar Nagar city is a significant landmark in the history of Kashmir and is considered one of the most important religious and cultural sites in the region. The mosque reflects the fusion of Hindu and Islamic architecture and is a testament to the region's rich cultural heritage.

Q. no.31 What is the significance of the Mughal Gardens of Kashmir?

Ans. The Mughal Gardens of Kashmir are significant for several reasons. They reflect the Mughal's love for nature and art and represent a fusion of different architectural styles. The gardens have also influenced garden design throughout the world and are considered a testament to the Mughal's legacy in Kashmir.

Q. no. 32 How have the Mughal Gardens of Kashmir influenced the culture of Kashmir?

Ans. The Mughal Gardens of Kashmir have had a significant impact on the culture of Kashmir and are considered an important part of the region's cultural heritage. The gardens have inspired poets, writers, and artists, and they continue to be an important tourist attraction in the region.

Q. no. 33 What is the significance of the Mughal Gardens of Kashmir in the context of environmental conservation?

Ans. The Mughal Gardens of Kashmir are significant in the context of environmental conservation as they represent a unique blend of human creativity and natural beauty. The gardens have been designed to incorporate natural elements, such as water channels and fountains, and are a testament to the Mughal's appreciation for the environment.

Medium Answer Type Questions

Q. no.1 Explain the history of Nagar Nagar city in Kashmir?

Ans. Nagar Nagar city is a historic town located in the Budgam district of Kashmir, India. It has a rich history that dates back to ancient times, with references to the city in historical texts dating back to the 8th century. The city has been ruled by various dynasties throughout history, including the Mughals, the Sikhs, and the Dogras.

Q. no.2 Who were the founders of Nagar Nagar city?

Ans. The founders of Nagar Nagar city are unknown, as the city has been inhabited since ancient times. However, the city has been ruled by various dynasties throughout history, including the Mughals, who left a significant architectural and cultural legacy in the city.

Q. no.3 Can you describe the architectural style of Jamaia Masjid in Nagar Nagar city?

Ans. Jamia Masjid in Nagar Nagar city is an excellent example of Indo-Islamic architecture, which combines Hindu and Islamic elements. The mosque features a large courtyard and four minarets, as well as intricate carvings and decorations on its walls.

Q. no.4 Who was responsible for the design of the Mughal Gardens of Kashmir?

Ans. The Mughal Gardens of Kashmir were designed by a team of architects and landscape designers, including Ali Mardan Khan and Nur Jahan. The gardens were commissioned by the Mughal Emperor Jahangir in the early 17th century and were designed to reflect the Mughal's love for nature and art.

Q. no.5 What is the significance of the Mughal Gardens of Kashmir in the context of garden design history?

Ans. The Mughal Gardens of Kashmir are significant in the context of garden design history as they represent a fusion of different architectural styles and have influenced garden design throughout the world. The gardens incorporate natural elements, such as water features and the surrounding mountains, into the overall design, and are known for their use of symmetry, balance, and terraces.

Q. no. 6 What is the cultural significance of the Mughal Gardens of Kashmir?

Ans. The Mughal Gardens of Kashmir are an important part of the region's cultural heritage and have influenced the culture of Kashmir in various ways. The gardens have inspired poets, writers, and artists, and are considered an important tourist attraction in the region. They are also an important symbol of the Mughal legacy in Kashmir and a testament to their appreciation for nature and art.

Q. no.8 How have the Mughal Gardens of Kashmir contributed to environmental conservation?

Ans. The Mughal Gardens of Kashmir are significant in the context of environmental conservation as they represent a unique blend of human creativity and natural beauty. The gardens have been designed to incorporate natural elements, such as water channels and fountains, and are a testament to the Mughal's appreciation for the environment. They continue to be an important tourist attraction in the region and are an example of how human creativity can be used to enhance and preserve natural beauty.

Q. no. 9 What is the historical significance of Jamaia Masjid in Nagar Nagar city?

Ans. Jamaia Masjid in Nagar Nagar city is a historic mosque that dates back to the Mughal era. It was built by Emperor Aurangzeb in the 17th century and has served as a significant place of worship for the Muslim community in the region. The mosque is also significant for its architectural style, which reflects the fusion of Hindu and Islamic architectural elements.

Q. no.10 How did the Mughal Gardens of Kashmir contribute to the development of garden design in India?

Ans. The Mughal Gardens of Kashmir are significant in the development of garden design in India as they represent a unique blend of Persian, Central Asian, and Indian architectural styles. The gardens have influenced garden design in India and beyond, particularly in the use of water features, terracing, and symmetry. They are also known for their use of plant species and the creation of microclimates within the garden.

Q. no. 11 Can you tell me more about the Mughal Emperor Jahangir's involvement in the development of the Mughal Gardens of Kashmir?

Ans. Mughal Emperor Jahangir was instrumental in the development of the Mughal Gardens of Kashmir. He commissioned the gardens in the early 17th century as a tribute to his love for nature and art. Jahangir was involved in the design of the gardens, and he is said to have spent a significant amount of time in the gardens during his visits to Kashmir.

Q. no. 12 What is the cultural significance of Nagar Nagar city?

Ans. Nagar Nagar city is a significant cultural centre in Kashmir, known for its rich history, architecture, and traditional crafts. The city has been home to various dynasties throughout history, including the Mughals, the Sikhs, and the Dogras, and it has served as a significant centre for trade and commerce. The city is also known for its traditional handicrafts, including shawls, carpets, and embroidery.

Q. no.13 Can you describe the architectural style of the Mughal Gardens of Kashmir?

Ans. The Mughal Gardens of Kashmir feature a unique blend of Persian, Central Asian, and Indian architectural styles. They are known for their use of water features, including fountains, channels, and pools, as well as their use of terracing and symmetry. The gardens are also famous for their use of plant species, including fruit trees, cypress trees, and roses, and for their creation of microclimates within the garden.

Q. no. 14 How have the Mughal Gardens of Kashmir contributed to the tourism industry in the region?

Ans. The Mughal Gardens of Kashmir are a significant tourist attraction in the region, and they have contributed to the development of the tourism industry in Kashmir. The gardens attract tourists from all over the world, and they are known for their natural beauty, architectural significance, and cultural heritage. The gardens have also contributed to the development of the hospitality industry in the region, with numerous hotels and resorts located in the vicinity of the gardens.

Q. no.15 What is the significance of the garden in Jama Masjid in Srinagar?

Ans. The garden in Jama Masjid is known as the Shahi Hamdan Garden and is an important feature of the mosque. The garden was named after Mir Sayyid Ali Hamdani, a renowned Sufi saint who played a key role in spreading Islam in the region. The garden is a beautiful oasis in the heart of the city and features a variety of trees and plants, including roses, cypress, and chinar trees. The garden is a popular spot for visitors who come to relax and enjoy the tranquillity of the surroundings.

Q. no.16 What are the features of the prayer hall in Jama Masjid in Srinagar?

Ans. The prayer hall of Jama Masjid is a grand structure with the capacity to accommodate thousands of worshippers at a time. The hall is built with red bricks and limestone and is supported by numerous pillars. The pillars are intricately carved with geometric designs and inscriptions from the Quran. The hall also features a high ceiling and a series of domes that enhance its aesthetic appeal. The mihrab, which indicates the direction of Mecca, is located at the center of the prayer hall.

Q. no. 17 What is the architecture of the Jamia Masjid in Srinagar?

Ans. Jama Masjid is a fine example of Islamic architecture, characterized by its spacious courtyard, tall minarets, and arched entrances. The mosque has a rectangular shape and is built with red bricks and limestone. It has a spacious prayer hall with the capacity to accommodate thousands of worshippers at a time. The mosque also has a beautiful garden, which adds to its aesthetic appeal.

Q. no.18 What is the history of Jama Masjid in Srinagar?

Ans. The construction of Jamia Masjid was started in 1394 CE during the reign of Sultan Sikander Shah Mir. It was completed in 1402 CE by his son, Sultan Zain-ul-Abidin. The mosque underwent several renovations and expansions during the centuries that followed, and it has been damaged and rebuilt multiple times due to various political and natural reasons.

Q. no.20 What are the Mughal Gardens in Kashmir, and how did they come to be?

Ans. Mughal Gardens is a group of historic gardens located in the Kashmir Valley, in the Indian-administered state of Jammu and Kashmir. The gardens were built by the Mughal emperors, who ruled over India during the 16th and 17th centuries. The gardens were built as a symbol of the Mughal Empire's grandeur and power and served as a retreat for the Mughal emperors during the hot summer months.

Q. no.21 What are the key features of the Mughal Gardens in Kashmir?

Ans. The Mughal Gardens in Kashmir are known for their stunning beauty and exquisite architecture. The gardens are characterized by terraced lawns, fountains, water channels, and ornamental trees and flowers. The gardens are also adorned with pavilions, pergolas, and other architectural features that add to their charm and elegance.

Long Answer Type Questions

Q. no.1 What is the history of Jama Masjid in Srinagar and what role has it played in the cultural and religious life of the region?

Ans. Jama Masjid in Srinagar is one of the most significant landmarks of the city, with a rich and storied history dating back to the 14th century. The mosque was built in 1394 CE by Sultan Sikandar Shah, who was the ruler of the Shah Miri dynasty that ruled over the Kashmir valley during that time. The mosque was built on the site of an earlier temple dedicated to the Hindu goddess, Sharika Devi, and the construction of the mosque marked the beginning of a new era in the history of the region.

The architecture of Jama Masjid is a blend of Persian and Islamic styles, with intricate carvings, ornate domes, and a spacious courtyard. The mosque has four minarets, each standing at a height of 140 feet, and a prayer hall that can accommodate over 30,000 worshippers at a time. The mosque also has a library that houses several rare and ancient manuscripts.

Over the centuries, Jama Masjid has played a significant role in the religious and cultural life of the people of Srinagar. The mosque has been a centre of learning and scholarship, with several renowned Islamic scholars and poets having studied and taught here. The mosque has also been a hub for social and philanthropic activities, such as providing food and shelter to the needy and supporting the education of the underprivileged.

During the reign of the Mughal emperor, Akbar, in the 16th century, Jama Masjid was renovated and expanded. The mosque underwent further renovations during the reign of the Afghan governor, Atta Mohammad Khan, in the 18th century, who added several new features to the mosque, such as the courtyard fountain and the ablution pool.

Jama Masjid has also been a witness to several historical events that have shaped the destiny of the region. During the Dogra rule in the 19th century, the mosque was the site of several protests and demonstrations against the oppressive policies of the rulers. The mosque was also a target of destruction during the devastating earthquake that struck the region in 1885, but it was subsequently restored to its former glory. However, efforts are being made to preserve and protect the mosque's heritage, with several restoration projects being undertaken to repair and maintain the mosque's structure and features.

Today, Jama Masjid stands as a symbol of the region's rich cultural and religious heritage, and it continues to be a vital part of the social and cultural fabric of the city. The mosque is a testament to the enduring legacy of the people of Srinagar, who have preserved and protected their cultural and religious heritage over the centuries.

Q. no.2 What efforts are being made to preserve and restore Jama Masjid in Srinagar?

Ans. Several efforts are being made to preserve and restore Jama Masjid to its former glory. The government of Jammu and Kashmir has allocated funds for the restoration of the mosque, and various conservation agencies have been involved in the process. The restoration work includes the repair of the mosque's infrastructure, such as the roofs, walls, and floors, as well as the restoration of its decorative features, such as intricate carvings and inscriptions. The restoration work is being carried out in a phased manner to ensure that the mosque remains accessible to visitors while the work is underway.

Q. no.3 How has Jama Masjid in Srinagar influenced the art and culture of the region?

Ans. Jama Masjid has played a significant role in promoting the art and literature of the region. It has been a centre of learning and spiritual discourse, where scholars and artists have gathered to exchange ideas and showcase their work. The mosque has also inspired many poets and writers to compose works that celebrate its grandeur and beauty. In addition, the mosque has hosted various cultural events and festivals, such as the annual Urs festival, which attracts a large number of visitors from different parts of the world.

Q. no.3 How have the Mughal Gardens in Kashmir impacted the region's tourism industry?

Ans. The Mughal Gardens in Kashmir is a major tourist attraction, and their stunning beauty and cultural significance have helped to promote the region's tourism industry. The gardens attract thousands of visitors every year, who come to admire their grandeur and tranquillity. The gardens are also a popular venue for cultural and social events, such as weddings, picnics, and festivals, which add to their allure and charm.

Q. no.4 What steps are being taken to preserve and protect the Mughal Gardens in Kashmir?

Ans. The Mughal Gardens in Kashmir are facing several threats due to environmental degradation, natural disasters, and human activities. To preserve and protect these historic gardens, the government has undertaken several initiatives, such as restoring and repairing the gardens' structures, installing water conservation systems, and promoting sustainable tourism practices. Additionally, awareness campaigns are being conducted to educate people about the importance of preserving these iconic gardens for future generations.

Chapter-X

Short Answer Type Questions

Q. no.1 What is Medieval Architecture?

Ans. Medieval architecture refers to the architectural styles that were prevalent during the Middle Ages, from the 5th century to the 15th century.

Q. no.2 What is the historical value of Medieval Architecture?

Ans. Medieval architecture serves as a visual representation of the social, economic, and cultural development of the Middle Ages. It reflects the beliefs, values, and aspirations of the people of that time.

Q. no.3 What is the aesthetic value of Medieval Architecture?

Ans. Medieval architecture is valued for its unique features such as pointed arches, ribbed vaults, and flying buttresses. It is also admired for its intricate carvings, stained glass windows, and sculptures that depict religious and mythological themes.

Q. no.4 Why is Medieval Architecture important to study?

Ans. Studying Medieval Architecture helps us understand the cultural and artistic achievements of the past. It also allows us to appreciate the beauty and complexity of these architectural styles.

Q. no.6 What are some famous examples of Medieval Architecture in Kashmir?

Ans. Shah Hamdan Mosque, Pari Mahal, Jama Masjid, Khanqah-e-Moula and Hari Parbat Fort.

Q. no.7 How did Medieval Architecture influence later architectural styles?

Ans. Medieval Architecture had a significant impact on later architectural styles such as Gothic Revival and Renaissance. Elements of Medieval Architecture can be seen in many modern buildings, particularly in churches and government buildings.

Q. no.8 What were some of the challenges faced by Medieval architects and builders?

Ans. Medieval architects and builders faced several challenges, including limited resources, lack of technology, and inadequate tools. They had to rely on their creativity and expertise to construct buildings that were sturdy and aesthetically pleasing.

Q. no.9 What were some of the key features of Medieval Castles?

Ans. Medieval castles were characterized by their thick walls, towers, and moats. They were designed to protect their occupants from enemy attacks.

Q. no.10 What role did religion play in Medieval Architecture?

Ans. Religion played a significant role in Medieval Architecture. Churches and cathedrals were designed as places of worship and reflection. The architecture of these buildings reflected the religious beliefs and values of the people of that time.

Q. no.11 How has the preservation of Medieval Architecture been important?

Ans. The preservation of Medieval Architecture has been important in maintaining our cultural heritage. It allows us to learn from the past and appreciate the achievements of our ancestors. It also provides a visual representation of our history and identity.

Q.no.12 What were some of the popular building materials used in Medieval Architecture?

Ans. The popular building materials used in Medieval Architecture were stone, brick, and timber. These materials were readily available and were used to construct sturdy and durable buildings.

Q. no.13 What was the role of guilds in Medieval Architecture?

Ans. Guilds played a significant role in Medieval Architecture. They were associations of craftsmen who worked together to maintain high standards of workmanship and protect their trade secrets. They also provided training and support to new apprentices.

Q. no.14 What were some of the key advancements in Medieval Architecture?

Ans. Some of the key advancements in Medieval Architecture included the development of pointed arches, ribbed vaults, and flying buttresses. These innovations allowed for the construction of larger and more complex buildings.

Q. no.15 What is the current state of Medieval Architecture?

Ans. Many Medieval buildings still exist today, although some have suffered damage over time. Preservation efforts are ongoing to ensure that these buildings are maintained and protected for future generations to enjoy.

Q. no.16 Write a note on the medieval architecture of Kashmir.

Ans. The medieval architecture of Kashmir is a reflection of the region's rich cultural and artistic heritage. It includes a range of styles, such as Persian, Islamic, and Indian, and features impressive structures like mosques, shrines, forts, and gardens. Some famous examples of medieval architecture in Kashmir are the Shah Hamdan Mosque, Pari Mahal, Jama Masjid, Khanqah-e-Moula, and Hari Parbat Fort. These structures are known for their intricate carvings, elegant wooden architecture, and strategic locations. They serve as a testament to Kashmir's vibrant past and continue to be an important part of the region's cultural identity.

Medium Answer Type Questions

Q. no.1 What is Medieval Architecture?

Ans. Medieval architecture refers to the architectural styles that were prevalent during the Middle Ages, from the 5th century to the 15th century. It encompasses a wide range of architectural styles, including Romanesque, Gothic, and Renaissance, which were characterized by specific design elements, construction techniques, and materials.

Q. no.2 What is the historical value of Medieval Architecture?

Ans. Medieval architecture has significant historical value as it provides a visual representation of the social, economic, and cultural development of the Middle Ages. The architectural styles of this period were influenced by the political and religious climate of the time, as well as by the available technology and resources. The buildings constructed during this period reflect the beliefs, values, and aspirations of the people of that time.

Q. no.3 What is the aesthetic value of Medieval Architecture?

Ans. Medieval architecture has great aesthetic value, as it is characterized by unique features such as pointed arches, ribbed vaults, and flying buttresses. The intricate carvings, stained glass windows, and sculptures that depict religious and mythological themes are also admired for their beauty and artistic quality. The overall effect of these architectural styles is to create a sense of grandeur, majesty, and spirituality.

Q. no.4 Why is Medieval Architecture important to study?

Ans. Studying Medieval Architecture is important for several reasons. Firstly, it helps us understand the cultural and artistic achievements of the past. By examining the architectural styles and techniques of the Middle Ages, we can gain insight into the social, political, and religious values of that time. Secondly, it allows us to appreciate the beauty and complexity of these architectural styles. Finally, it provides a foundation for understanding the evolution of later architectural styles.

Q. no.5 What are some famous examples of Medieval Architecture?

Ans. There are many famous examples of Medieval Architecture, including the Notre Dame Cathedral in Paris, Westminster Abbey in London, and the Colosseum in Rome. These buildings are admired for their beauty, historical significance, and cultural importance. They serve as a testament to the ingenuity, creativity, and skill of the architects and builders who constructed them.

Q. no.6 How did Medieval Architecture influence later architectural styles?

Ans. Medieval Architecture had a significant impact on later architectural styles such as Gothic Revival and Renaissance. The design elements and construction techniques developed during the Middle Ages served as a foundation for the development of new styles and approaches to architecture. Elements of Medieval Architecture can be seen in many modern buildings, particularly in churches and government buildings.

Q. no.7 What were some of the challenges faced by Medieval architects and builders?

Ans. Medieval architects and builders faced several challenges when constructing buildings during the Middle Ages. These challenges included limited resources, lack of technology, and inadequate tools. Builders had to rely on their creativity and expertise to construct buildings that were sturdy and aesthetically pleasing. The use of new construction techniques and materials, such as pointed arches and ribbed vaults, helped overcome some of these challenges.

Q. no.8 What were some of the key features of Medieval Castles?

Ans. Medieval castles were characterized by their thick walls, towers, and moats. They were designed to protect their occupants from enemy attacks. Castles also included features such as drawbridges, portcullises, and battlements to further enhance their defensive capabilities.

Q. no.9 What role did religion play in Medieval Architecture?

Ans. Religion played a significant role in Medieval Architecture. Churches and cathedrals were designed as places of worship and reflection. The architecture of these buildings reflected the religious beliefs and values of the people of that time. Religious themes were often depicted in the decoration of these buildings, with sculptures and stained glass windows depicting scenes from the Bible and other religious texts.

Q. no.10 What were some of the popular building materials used in Medieval Architecture?

Ans. The popular building materials used in Medieval Architecture were stone, brick, and timber. These materials were readily available and were used to construct sturdy and durable buildings. Stone was particularly popular for its durability, while brick and timber were used for their ease of use and availability.

Q. no.11 What was the role of guilds in Medieval Architecture?

Ans. Guilds played a significant role in Medieval Architecture. They were associations of craftsmen who worked together to maintain high standards of workmanship and protect their trade secrets. They also provided training and support to new apprentices. Guilds were particularly important in the construction of churches and cathedrals, as they helped ensure that the buildings were constructed to a high standard.

Q. no.12 What were some of the key advancements in Medieval Architecture?

Ans. Some of the key advancements in Medieval Architecture included the development of pointed arches, ribbed vaults, and flying buttresses. These innovations allowed for the construction of larger and more complex buildings. Pointed arches allowed for taller and more slender buildings, while ribbed vaults provided additional support for the roof. Flying buttresses allowed for greater stability in large buildings.

Q. no.13 What was the significance of Gothic Architecture in Medieval times?

Ans. Gothic Architecture was significant in Medieval times as it represented a shift from the Romanesque style. Gothic buildings were characterized by their intricate decoration and emphasis on vertical lines. They were also designed to allow more natural light into the building. The gothic architecture reflected the religious and cultural values of the time and was used to express the power and wealth of the church.

Q. no.14 What is the current state of Medieval Architecture?

Ans. Many Medieval buildings still exist today, although some have suffered damage over time. Preservation efforts are ongoing to ensure that these buildings are maintained and protected for future generations to enjoy. Many Medieval buildings have been repurposed for modern use, such as museums or government buildings, while others continue to serve their original purpose as places of worship.

Long Answer Type Questions

Q. no.1 What is the historical significance of Medieval Architecture?

Ans. Medieval Architecture has significant historical value as it reflects the social, religious, and cultural values of the time. In the Middle Ages, the church was a central part of daily life, and church buildings were often the most important and impressive structures in towns and cities. The architecture of these buildings, particularly the grand cathedrals, was used to express the power and wealth of the church.

Medieval Architecture also reflects the advances in engineering and construction techniques of the time. The development of pointed arches, ribbed vaults, and flying buttresses allowed for the construction of larger and more complex buildings than had been possible before. The use of these techniques also allowed for the creation of buildings with more intricate and decorative features, such as stained glass windows and elaborate carvings.

Additionally, Medieval Architecture has historical value as it reflects the political and economic structures of the time. Many Medieval buildings, particularly castles and fortresses, were designed for defence purposes. The architecture of these buildings reflects the feudal system, with the lord's residence often being the most impressive and well-fortified structure in the area.

Q. no.2 What is the aesthetic value of Medieval Architecture?

Ans. Medieval Architecture has significant aesthetic value due to its intricate decoration, use of light and shadow, and focus on verticality. Gothic Architecture, in particular, is known for its ornate decoration and intricate carvings. The use of stained glass windows allowed for the creation of a stunning interplay between light and shadow, creating a sense of otherworldliness and beauty.

Additionally, the use of verticality in Medieval Architecture creates a sense of grandeur and awe. Many Medieval buildings, particularly cathedrals, were designed to reach towards the heavens, with soaring spires and pointed arches. This emphasis on vertical lines creates a sense of upward movement and aspiration, reinforcing the religious and cultural values of the time.

Finally, Medieval Architecture also has aesthetic value due to the skill and craftsmanship required to create these buildings. The intricate carvings and delicate stonework required a level of skill and attention to detail that is often lacking in modern construction. The preservation of these buildings allows us to appreciate the skill and craftsmanship of the medieval craftsmen who created them.

Q. no.3 How does the debate on the value of Medieval Architecture reflect wider cultural and historical debates?

Ans. The debate on the value of Medieval Architecture reflects wider cultural and historical debates around the role of history in contemporary society. Some argue that the preservation of medieval buildings is important for cultural and historical reasons, as they represent an important part of our shared heritage. They argue that the destruction or neglect of these buildings would be a loss to our collective cultural memory.

Others argue that the preservation of Medieval buildings is a waste of resources and that these buildings should be allowed to fall into disrepair or be demolished to make way for more modern structures. They argue that the historical value of these buildings is overstated and that they have little relevance to modern society.

This debate reflects wider discussions around the value of tradition and history in contemporary society. Some argue that tradition and history are important for creating a sense of identity and continuity, while others argue that they can be oppressive and limit progress. The debate around the value of Medieval Architecture is an important part of these wider discussions, as it reflects the tensions between tradition and progress and the role of the past in shaping our present and future.

* 9 7 8 9 3 5 6 6 7 8 5 1 4 *